GLOBALIZATION, NON-FORMAL EDUCATION AND RURAL DEVELOPMENT

GLOBALIZATION, NON-FORMAL EDUCATION AND RURAL DEVELOPMENT IN DEVELOPING ECONOMIES

ALBERT D. K. AMEDZRO

Senior Resident Tutor, Institute of Adult Education, University of Ghana, Legon

GHANA UNIVERSITIES PRESS
ACCRA
2005

Published by
Ghana Universities Press
P. O. Box GP 4219
Accra
Tel: 233(21) 513401, 513404
Fax: 233(21) 513402
E-mail: ghanauniversitiespress@yahoo.com

ISBN: 9-9643034-24

PRODUCED IN GHANA
Typesetting by Ghana Universities Press, Accra
Printing and binding by Yamens Press Limited, Accra

To

SAMUEL SALIFU MOGRE

for his selfless and unparalleled devotion to the cause of non-formal education in Ghana.

CONTENTS

FOREWORD

Despite the euphoria that accompanied political independence and the several attempts made in the 1960s and 1970s to introduce grandiose development programmes, many African, and indeed, most developing countries entered the 1990s with the stark realization that there had been a reduction in the standard of living of their populations. Developing countries are in more serious problems at the advent of the current trend of globalization. Political instability, social deprivation and economic turbulence deny these countries the opportunity to actively participate in the process. The majority of people and especially those in the rural areas are marginalized and cannot participate in the development process.

Two of the pervasive problems these countries are currently faced with as they seek functional linkage with the outside world in the face of globalization are the problems of unemployment and increasing urbanization, the latter in particular leading to deteriorating conditions of living and reduced agricultural production. The consequences of both have been devastating, and the need to address them in national development schemes has become very imperative.

The author has carefully analyzed the causes and consequences of these two hydra-headed phenomena in developing countries, using carefully selected data from Ghana, and has proffered *Non-Formal Education* as a strategy for mitigating these problems.

The book reviews the results attained by non-formal education programmes that used the Freirean approach in particular in developing relevant functional education in Tanzania, and succeeded to some extent, in retaining the youth in the rural areas. The author argues that non-formal education programmes and institutions offer the best prospects for meaningful development in poor nations. Through an analysis of the Ghana National Functional Literacy Programme, the author shows the potentialities for change through the introduction of Non-Formal Education.

The analysis shows how literacy can be used as the fulcrum for development and highlights factors that can accelerate literacy and the development process in any national programme. The author concedes that a national educational programme is not easy to promote in any country, but such problems are global, and can be understood if national examples are studied. It is with that understanding that the close, critical appraisal of the Ghana performance can be appreciated.

Outlining the various concrete forms in which non-formal education has been translated, the author dilates on how the functional literacy programme is helping to improve the knowledge, skills and attitudes of the hitherto marginalized segment of the population. It is helping isolated rural communities become more articulate and helping individuals acquire skills to generate income. The book provides a comprehensive description of how non-formal education was operationalized in Ghana and identifies how the mass media in particular, such as community newspapers and popular theatre were used to educate individual communities and mobilize them to participate not only in their own development but also in the global process.

As stated earlier, this book could not have come at a more opportune time when all developing countries have shown signs that human-centred development is now their goal. It will prove most valuable to both the policy-maker and the social/community development practitioner. The language used is clear, simple and lucid, and I have no doubt that it makes very significant contribution to the discussion of strategies which can prove most efficacious in the development of the relatively new nations of Africa to ensure their participation in the global process.

The book succeeds most significantly in understanding the relationship between development and functional literacy, using Ghana's case as a researchable example or model. I recommend it as compulsory reading for all those who have to deal with development in primary communities.

PROFESSOR KOBINA ASIEDU
Director, Institute of Adult Education
University of Ghana, Legon

ACKNOWLEDGEMENT

I owe a lot of gratitude to many people in the production of this work. I wish to mention only a few: Mr. R. A. Banibensu, Dr. Dan Oduro-Mensah and Mr. C. C. K. Dzakpasu all of the Institute of Adult Education, who corrected the draft and gave me many useful suggestions. I cannot forget to mention Mrs. Evelyn Appiah-Donyina, of the Institute of Adult Education, my academic adviser, who continues to encourage me to develop my manuscripts, including this book which she has critically edited. I owe her the millennium gratitude.

I am also grateful to Professor Kobina Asiedu, my Director who also critically assessed the book and provided the foreword. I appreciate the patience of Miss Pauline Kumdah, Mr. William W. K. Vitashie and Miss Gifty Brew-Sam who neatly typed the script.

May I place on record the financial support given to me by my younger brother, Mr. Robert K. Amedzro, the Managing Director of Universal Chemists Ltd., Accra, which enabled me to produce this work.

I admire my wife Maggie Mamasco and my children for tolerating the time I was absent from home during the writing of this book.

Chapter 1

GLOBALIZATION

Introduction

The motivation for this book is to give the reader a global picture of the challenges, omissions and potentials regarding the chequered process of rural development in the globalized developing economies. It is also to highlight some of the structural weaknesses of many a Third World economy, illustrating the structural deficiencies characteristic of peripheral capitalism in the developing nations. These deficiencies obstruct the successful implementation of rural development blueprints. They distort linkages between the formal and informal sectors of the developing national economies. They also hinder the efforts of the South to scientifically develop and actively participate in global economic activities.

Since the 1970s and especially, from 1973 when the price of oil quadrupled, development in the South has been in a more serious crisis. In Sub-Saharan Africa the provision of social services slowed down. The economy staggered and hunger became real. Conditions worsened in the 1980s.

After the fall of the Union of Soviet Socialist Republics (USSR) in 1991, the United States of America (USA) and European countries made conscious efforts to revitalize the concept of globalization. By this strategy, all countries, both in the North and South are to develop, trade and work together. It is against this background that the discussion in this book starts with the concept of globalization, illustrating some of the structures and conditions that enhance or limit its success. Political instability, economic structural deficiencies, youth unemployment and low community participation in the development process are identified as some of the factors limiting developing countries from actively participating in the globalizing trends. The later two factors are discussed in more detail. It is believed that when developing countries motivate

1

people to take part in their own development and effectively tackle the problem of rural development, the global process will pick up.

Among other strategies, many developing countries have adopted non-formal education as a decisive instrument in rural development. Some non-formal education institutions in the traditional system are also discussed to show their viability in the modern rural development process. Comparative experiences in non-formal education strategies from Brazil, Tanzania and more particularly from Ghana are illustrated as examples in the rural development process.

The Concept of Globalization

According to the *Cambridge International Dictionary of English* (1997), globalization refers to the process of operating internationally. Explaining the concept further, Lockard (1999) noted that, "the term globalization refers to the increasing inter connectedness of nations and people around the world through trade, investment, travel, popular culture, and other forms of interaction" (Lockard 1999 : 1).

Globalization implies integration among all countries of the world. In other words, all countries are assumed to have perceived the need to participate actively together in the affairs of the world. The process is facilitated by innovations in communication technology such as the internet, television, travel opportunities and investment in overseas countries. Tourist attractions, scattered all over the world, also enhance the modern globalization process. Briefly put, globalization is a process of integrating the governance, economy, culture, science and technology across national boundaries. This means that the political, economic, technological and social structures and activities of countries are improved and linked together. Stronger ties are built among all states in all spheres of life. The greatest driving force, however, is the economic factor facilitated mainly by the use of the American dollar (US$). The essence of globalization is to promote the holistic development of all countries for the benefit of mankind globally. All countries are now, therefore, making conscious efforts to develop themselves so that they

2

can actively participate in the process. Globalization is now a revolution shaping the world.

Origins of Globalization

Lockard (1999) asserts that globalization is not a new phenomenon. It existed long ago but picked up between 1000 and 1500 AD. This was the period when a very active long distance trade existed among the people of Asia. There was an intensive and very extensive interaction among countries bordering the Indian Ocean and the South China Sea, the most dynamic regions in the world at that time.

The most important trade on land for many centuries as Lockard pointed out was the silk trade through Central Asia. There was also the maritime trade on the Indian Ocean, which was patronized heavily by the Muslims who spread their culture and influence in the entire eastern hemisphere. The Chinese also actively participated in the trading activities leading to the spread of Afro-Euro Asian civilization and globalized economy and culture. The trade, especially the silk trade, expanded to cover trade in porcelain and bamboo from China to Baghdad and the Mediterranean ports, Italy, India and Europe. Trading centres which became globalized entrepôts for commerce and culture became vibrant. One such important trading centre then was the port of Melaka in Malaya. In the period between 1000 and 1500 AD, the sea trade became more lucrative than the overland silk trade. Trading activities brought Arabia, Persia and India and East Africa into close contact.

In the same period, various attempts were made by some religious groups also to bring the world together. The Muslims and especially, the Almoravids spread their Islamic influence in Asia and northern and western Africa. The Christian religion was also spread in the world, reaching the Gold Coast (now Ghana) in 1529.

Then came the period of the scramble for and partition and colonization of Africa and other parts of the world by European countries. Peace existed in the world till 1914 when the First World War broke out. After the First World War, the League of Nations was established in 1918 to prevent the outbreak of another world war. The rationale was to bring the world together peacefully under the umbrella

3

of the League. Unfortunately, however, the Second World War broke out in 1939.

When the war ended, the United Nations Organization (UN) was established in 1945 to maintain peace among the people of the world. Among other purposes, the UN is

- — to maintain international peace;
- — to develop friendly relations among nations;
- — to achieve international co-operation in solving international economic, social, cultural or humanitarian problems and in encouraging respect for human rights and fundamental freedom for all;
- — to be a centre for harmonizing the actions of nations in attaining these common ends (UNO 1971: 5).

It was envisaged that the world would live at peace and develop together under the UN. It was in view of the above that the UN established six main organs to deal with world issues. These six organs include the General Assembly which is the main deliberative organ of the UN on world issues. The Security Council is to settle disputes among states, keep international peace and security and order military or economic sanction against any aggressor. The Economic and Social Council is charged with the responsibility to direct and promote the economic and social activities of members. The Trusteeship Council is charged to administer and supervise territories placed under the UN after the war. The International Court of Justice at The Hague in the Netherlands is the principal judicial organ of the UN. It settles all legal issues brought before it, while the Secretariat is a co-coordinating unit among the councils and functions as the administrative machinery for the UN (UNO *ibid.*).

In order to promote the socio-economic development of all countries, the United Nations Organization established some structures like the United Nations Development Programme, (UNDP) the United Nations Conference on Trade and Development (UNCTAD), the United Nations Industrial Development Organization (UNIDO), the World

Food Programme (WFP) and the United Nations Children's Fund (UNICEF). There are some agencies related to the United Nations which help developing countries to improve upon their development programmes. These include the International Labour Organization (ILO), the Food and Agriculture Organization (FAO), United Nations Educational, Scientific and Cultural Organization (UNESCO), the World Health Organization (WHO) and the International Monetary Fund (IMF).

It would appear that the fortunes of the UN and the globalization process were, however, limited by the cold war. The twenty-five years that proceeded the Second World War (1945–1970) witnessed the Cold War between the USSR and its allies on the one hand and the United States (US) and its allies on the other. The socialist theories of Karl Marx were adopted by USSR and its allies while the US and the West used the capitalist philosophy for development. Under these different theories, each nation-state pursued its own national system in the international economy. There was competition among states to promote foreign trade, to increase their wealth, influence and power no matter the dangers posed by these trade systems. The world was supposedly divided into three main sub-worlds: the First World was made up of the capitalist West, the Second of the socialist countries and the Third comprised the non-developed world in the south.

Modern Globalizing Trends

By 1991, USSR, a nuclear superpower, had become an isolated giant. It could neither balance its economy that was fast collapsing nor pay its debts. Already, the economies of Thailand, Indonesia and Malaysia all in the East, were in trouble. There was also a currency crisis in Brazil. The signs indicated that a new economic order had to be put in place otherwise the economies of other countries especially, in the eastern bloc would collapse. This was a challenge to both economists and politicians to adjust reality to a new global order as happened in the 19th century with the beginning of the Industrial Revolution.

With the collapse of the socialist/communist system at the beginning of the 1990s, the new global economy has developed at an

5

unprecedented rate. In his first inaugural address on January 20, 1993, President Bill Clinton, among other issues, touched on globalization of trade and foreign policy. He explained that "there is no longer any division between what is foreign and what is domestic — the world economy, the world environment, the world HIV/AIDS crisis, the world arms race — they affect us all.... Clearly, America must continue to lead the world we did so much to make" (Microsoft 1999:2, Bill Clinton's First Inaugural Address).

The entire world is brought into the new global market. Many entrepreneurs raise capital anywhere in the world, use technology, communication and labour no matter the location, to produce goods and services which are sold anywhere in the world. The world has become one market and the idea of nation-state is not so much pronounced in international affairs. The market economic competition is regulated by global trends and economic activities, which influence the policies of national union members forcing states to participate in the free global market. Countries have no choice but to liberalise their trade. Geographical barriers like the Mediterranean Sea, the Indian and Atlantic Oceans and River Rio Grand were no longer barriers to globalization. The era of social, political and economic revolution emerged (Longworth 1999).

Since nations have lost their absolute sovereignty in the process, they are now joining regional trade groupings to enable them take part effectively in the global market. They also adopt new currencies to cope with the change. Consequently, in January 1999, 15 European Union Members introduced the *Euro,* a common currency. The North American Free Trade Agreement was signed among the United States, Canada and Mexico to remove trade barriers and tariffs to most Latin American nations. In West Africa, the concept of Economic Community of West African States is strengthened to promote trading activities among members. The idea of introducing a new currency, the *Eco,* is proposed. In place of national governments, international bodies like the International Monetary Fund (IMF), World Trade Organization (WTO), and Bank for International Settlements in Switzerland are regulating the global economic order.

The multinational corporations which until recently established their sales and manufacturing branches all over the world but administered them directly from their headquarters had to review their operations and administrative strategies. Now, they have become global corporations with a skeleton staff at headquarters and the major administrative duties such as research, development, accounting, procurement and sales are performed in their offices wherever they operate in the world. According to Longworth (1999) there are as many as 50,000 such global corporations in the world. Some of these corporations he mentioned included the Ford Motor Company, General Motor Corporation, Royal Dutch/Shell Group, Nestle and Zenith Electronics Corporation.

There are several other factors that facilitate the globalization process as discussed by Longworth (1999). One of the factors mentioned by him is the explosion of the communication revolution including information technology. It was because of communication technology that Marshall McLuhan stated that the world was becoming a global village. It is important to note that the rate of revolution in communication technology increased substantially in the manufacture of transport, railway, telegraph, telephones, radio and motion pictures in the 19th century. The communication revolution was greatly enhanced in the 20th century with the expansion of the media, the production of a variety of motorcars and the aeroplane, with the invention of television and the computer, the latter in the 1960s. Since then communication technology has assumed more important dimensions.

With the introduction of the computer, the concept of "information society" has gained currency. Instant global communication especially by entrepreneurs has become possible. Sending messages to any part of the world at anytime is possible. The Stock Exchange transactions in Tokyo or New York are observed all over the world and pose an instant challenge to entrepreneurs and countries to adjust accordingly. The television, an information superhighway, has created a network of information flow throughout the world.

Through the Internet and the television, packages of information, entertainment and education are made available to many people no matter the distance and location. The communication revolution has brought the package not only to libraries but also homes, offices and communities. Homes are stocked with a variety of current books, magazines, newspapers, cassettes, videos and other gadgets like the radio, compact disc, record players, typewriters both electronic and manual, cameras, e-mail, fax, television and projectors (Briggs 1999). Homes are linked to the global world instantly.

As a result, national issues have turned out to be global concerns. The events in Kosovo and the arrest of General Augusto Pinochet in London and his repatriation and trial in Chile as a former dictator have become international issues. The crisis in Sierra Leone and the execution of Saro Wiwa and eight others in Nigeria, which one might think were internal affairs, have become big global issues. So also did the troubles in Yugoslavia become international issues. International financial sanctions and travel restrictions were imposed on Yugoslavia until President Milosevic was removed in October, 2000 and replaced by a democratically elected government headed by President Vojisla Kostunica. Moreover, the outbreak of violence in the Middle East between Israel and Palestine has led to an increase in oil price in the whole world.

Another important factor enhancing globalization is the deregulation of economic activities. According to Longworth (1999), before the late 1970s governments controlled imports and the flow of currencies. These were regulated by laws, tariffs and quotas by different governments. From the late 1970s, countries have been forced to deregulate economic activities so that markets could function effectively. This was the origin of the liberalization policy adopted by many countries. Foreign investments have now become more lucrative than trade. Western countries are investing heavily in the less developed countries.

This had been the case in Asian countries like Indonesia, Thailand, Malaysia, Singapore and Hong Kong where they invited foreign investors and liberalized their trade. These countries could no longer control their trading activities and the Western powers found this arrangement profitable. They made huge profits from cheap labour and cheap raw materials in the developing countries.

Yet another prominent factor enhancing globalization was the growth of large viable capital markets all over the world from the 1970s. Earlier on, in 1944 at the international Bretton Woods Conference, national currencies were assigned a fixed exchange rate against the United States dollar and supported by gold. With the collapse of the Bretton Woods system in 1973, many currencies began to be unstable and "floated" against the dollar. This trend has serious implications for the developing countries, as their currencies can not compete favourably with those of the developed countries. Markets determined the worth of each currency at any particular time. This was the origin of great global capital markets (Longworth *Ibid.*).

Schools of Thought on Globalization

Two major schools of thought have become prominent in the wake of globalization. The first is the Cornucopian School of Thought. This school believes that fast and high large-scale technological and economic development leads to the total enjoyment and happiness of all mankind and that it holds great promise for the survival of the world. Globalization, it is believed, would lead to the development of all countries. The second is the Doomsters School of Thought, which sees globalization in another light. It believes that globalization will further widen the development gap between the "Haves" (the developed world) and the "Have-Nots" (the developing world). As a result, the world will face a disaster: while the Haves develop at a faster rate the Have-Nots will be faced with exploitation, poverty, low wages and unemployment.

There are as many as 188 countries which are members of the United Nations Organization (UNO). They all have common characteristics such as the existence of a government, a currency and security forces. They all participate in international conferences and the General Assembly of the UN. But, as will be shown later, some of them are trapped by some challenges which prevent their active participation in the global process as noted by the Doomsters.

The capacity of people in the developing world must be built to widen opportunities for them to participate in the process. Women especially, who in many countries have been denied the opportunity to participate in the process are to be empowered to do so. Women and men as well should have access to education and information to understand and analyze social, economic and political issues so that they can know their rights and perform their roles responsibly. Globalization demands that all countries have to work together so that nobody becomes a casualty. It is in view of the above that certain structures have been put in place both by the developed and the developing worlds to meet the challenges of globalization.

SOME STRUCTURES OF GLOBALIZATION

Trade and Economic Support

In the economic field, an institution like the World Trade Organization has been strengthened to remove trade barriers among countries and to open trade avenues to developing countries. It has been realized by the developed countries that it is not enough to give aid to developing countries. Many world organizations such as the World Bank, the United Nations Development Programme and other non-governmental organizations like the Friedrich Ebert Foundation give financial and material support to developing countries to promote sustainable long-term socio-economic development. Japan is supporting Kenyan projects like the rehabilitation of Nyali and Mtwapa bridges so as to facilitate the movement of people and goods. It is also giving both financial and technical assistance to China to revive its economy.

The International Fund for Agricultural Development (IFAD) and the Sasakawa Global 2000 Project are also providing resources to revamp the agricultural sector of the Ghanaian economy which has a great potential for expansion. The European Union (EU) according to the *Daily Graphic* of 22nd September, 2000 has spent $125million so far on various micro-economic development projects in Ghana. The amount has been spent on the development of human resource, the private sector and the control of cocoa diseases. Similar structures and

10

support have been provided to bridge the economic gap between the developed and developing world.

Global Environmental Improvement

An area of global concern to countries is degradation and pollution of the environment. Attempts are, therefore, made by organizations to revegetate the world and control global warming. One such serious attempt was made at a recent UN forum held in September, 2000. The Religious Alliance and Convention (RAC) at the UN forum raised the issue of forging a network among religious groups and governments all over the world to tackle global warming and climatic change issues. Governments have been called upon by RAC to enforce the 1997 Kyoto Protocol of the UN Framework Convention on Climatic Change. By this Protocol, industrialized countries are to limit the emissions of gases from their machines which contribute to global warming, by five percent by 2008. Countries have been encouraged and supported to establish national agencies to promote environmental improvement activities. In Ghana, the Environmental Protection Agency has been established to check environmental degradation and pollution.

World Peace and Good Governance

Globalization is concerned with universal peace, good governance and democratic institutions. The United Nations, therefore, deploys peacekeeping forces in crisis situations for example, in the Middle East, Ethiopia and Eritrea. In Sierra Leone alone, the strength of the UN peacekeeping force was 13,000 soldiers by the end of August 2000. The United Nations High Commission for Refugees (UNHCR) takes care of war victims including refugees. The UN promotes democratic reforms in the whole world. It sends observers to ensure free and fair elections all over the world. Governments are prevailed upon to hold democratic elections on schedule and hand over power as appropriate. Heads of state whose terms of office expire have to retire constitutionally and hand over power to democratically elected governments on schedule. Material and financial resources are, therefore, given to developing countries by the developed world to support them conduct elections under observers and develop democratic structures.

There are global activities organized to unite nations and enhance peace and popular participation in the globalization process. One such important activity is the UN Summit in New York. Every year at the summit all members take stock of and formulate development plans. The Millennium Summit was held in the second week of September 2000. At this 55th General Assembly of the UN, it was reported that over 1,500 participants including Kings, Presidents and Prime Ministers were present. The leaders represented business, government and civil society interests. The summit highlighted the social implications of globalization, economic productivity and sustainability as well as spiritual and ethical challenges of globalization. It also suggested a more effective networking system among all countries to ensure and enhance a fair and positive industrialization, information technology and economic development. The summit offered stakeholders in globalization the opportunity to meet face to face and exchange ideas.

According to a Ghanaian newspaper, the *Daily Graphic* (9th September, 2000) the forum offered the opportunity to the US President, Bill Clinton and the Cuban Leader, Fidel Castro to shake hands and exchange a few words. The paper described this handshake as historic since this was the first time a US President shook hands with Fidel Castro since the Cuban leader took over power about four decades ago.

Debt Relief

Many developing countries have been saddled with huge debts owed to the developed countries. They are, therefore, unable to participate in the global market. In view of the above, at the Group of Seven (G7) summit in Cologne in 1998 and again in Japan in 1999, the G7 pledged to give debt relief packages to the world's poorest countries. Uganda has benefited from such a package. Spain has relieved Morocco of $40 million debt and in addition has donated $50 million to the latter to develop its infrastructure and fight poverty. The World Bank and the International Monetary Fund (IMF) have agreed to support a comprehensive debt reduction package for Cameroon. This is to enable her to develop her healthcare, primary education and HIV/AIDS prevention programmes. Similar support packages have been made available to many developing nations by the developed countries.

In Ghana, inflationary pressure mounted as a result of the lighter fiscal and monetary management because of the 1992, 1996 and 2000 general elections. According to the World Bank Report (2002:13), "fiscal loosening leading up to the 2000 elections exacerbated the problem and the Cedi lost half of its value in 2000 with the inflation rate reaching the 40 percent range for the first few months of 2001"

Already in 1996, the World Bank and the International Monetary Fund proposed the Highly Indebted Poor Country (HIPC) Initiative to reduce the external debt of the most indebted countries. The inflationary pressure prompted the Ghana government to apply for the Initiative in April, 2001. Support for Ghana under the Initiative was endorsed by the IDA and IMF in February, 2002. Under the Initiative, Ghana is to get a relief of US$ 3.700 million from her creditors and US$ 1.446 million from IDA to be spread over a 20 year period (World Bank, 2002) when Ghana attained the HIPC completion point successfully in July, 2004.

Involvement of Women in National and Global Issues

Until the 1970s, social and cultural constraints in many parts of the world excluded women from the model of development. They were relegated to the background; they performed domestic chores or menial jobs and did clerical work in offices. These constraints did not allow them to communicate with the outside world. The active participation of women in the development process is a new phenomenon. Since the last decade many important world organizations like the World Bank, the UNICEF and non-governmental organizations such as Oxfam have begun to support women's development programmes all over the world.

In 1995, a global conference of women was held in Beijing, China. The objective was to mobilize women and put their case across so that with men, they could be liberated from cultural norms to participate in the global process. Working documents on affirmative action to provide opportunities for women to take part in the social, economic and political spheres of society were prepared. The freedom from violence and women's participation in the development process have become key issues for women's organizations at the global level. The argument put forward by women is that, globalization means progress not only for men in the world but also for women. A global world should be a world free from inequality based on gender.

Many women organizations like the 31st December Women's Movement in Ghana have been formed. They are actively involved in fighting for women's rights and in organizing different types of socio-economic activities for members to liberate themselves from any type of slavery. They are now empowered to participate in national and international fora. Their president has been very vocal at many global conferences, fighting for women's rights.

The Olympic Games

One major activity in the world that brings all countries together is sports. The Olympic games, for example, are organized every four years for the whole world, where all kinds of games and sporting activities are undertaken. In the year 2000, the games took place in Sydney, Australia. All countries gathered together, stayed together, keenly competed together and learnt from one another: the idea being that of uniting the world through sports. The fact should not be lost on the reader that these games are viewed with excitement on the television the world over via satellite. So also are the World Cup football matches organized every four years to bring the world together through soccer.

Other Global Celebrations

Now that the world has become a global village, a number of activities and celebrations are more seriously organized for all countries to formulate and adopt common strategies and to harmonize their activities in the solution of problems. Some of the occasions celebrated together yearly are the World Food Day, the World Health Day, Teachers' Day,

World Literacy Day, World Environmental Day and the International Day of Peace. On the International Day of Peace, the Peace Bell is tolled outside the headquarters of the UN to draw world attention to the maintenance of global peace.

SOME PROBLEMS OF GLOBALIZATION

There are, however, many challenges to the process of globalization. There are vast discrepancies in the socio-economic and technological development of the developed and the developing world, thus dividing the world into two blocs. There is the developed North made up of Europe, Japan and North America and also the developing South totem-pole countries in Africa, Asia and Latin America. While political life in the North is comparatively stable, there are various degrees of political tension in the South. The border disputes between India and Pakistan have dragged on for many years. The 17-year war between the Islamic government in Sudan and the Sudan People's Liberation Army (SPLA) has no prospects of ending soon. The seven-year civil war in Burundi between the Tutsi-led army and the two main armed Hutu rebels groups (the Forces for the Defence of Democracy (FDD) and National Liberation Forces (NLF) has become a complicated issue. Kenya, Uganda and Rwanda are involved in the Burundi tension, trying to diffuse it. There is also the civil war in Rwanda.

The introduction of Sharia Law (Muslim Law) into States like Zamfara, Kaduna and Kano in Nigeria has brought political and social agitation to those states. Under this law, prostitutes are stoned, thieves have their hands cut off while drunkards are caned in public. In Nigeria again, the tension with religious connotations between the Hausas and the Yorubas broke out into violence in October 2000 resulting in the death of many people.

The once peaceful country, Côte d' Ivoire, is now sitting on a power keg after the death of President Houghet Boigny. In December, 1999, General Robert Guei, a retired army officer, toppled the constitutional government of President Henry Konan Bedie. The opposition leader, Alassane Ouattara a former Prime Minister of Côte d' Ivoire together with other 12 opposition leaders were prevented from standing in the presidential elections scheduled for October 2000. Tension mounted high in the country more particularly when an assassination attempt was made on the life of General Guei.

On the 22nd of October, 2000, controversial presidential elections were held. At the end of the elections both General Robert Guei and Laurent Gbagbo declared themselves winners. In the confusion that ensued General Guei had to flee the country. The votes were recounted and Gbagbo was declared winner and sworn into office on the 26th of October, 2000 amid protests from the supporters of Ouattara who himself sought refuge in the German ambassador's residence. For some time, Côte d'Ivorie became a land of confusion before and after the 2000 elections.

In Zimbabwe, the ejection of whites from their farms in the middle of 2000 was followed by tension between President Robert Mugabe's ruling ZANU-PF Party and the main opposition party, the Movement for Democratic Change (MDC) led by Morgan Tsvangirai. Rallies and demonstrations have been organized to make Mugabe step down peacefully or be forcefully removed from office before the 2002 scheduled presidential elections. Government raids on opposition offices have deepened the crisis in the country. Similarly, there are conflicts in Somalia, South Africa, Senegal, Morocco and Congo.

Ghana is comparatively a stable country but marked by sporadic ethnic conflicts between Alavanyo and Nkonya, Peki and Tsito in the 1990s and religious conflicts in the northern part of Ghana. More alarming were the conflicts between the Kokombas on one hand and the Nanumbas, the Gonjas, the Dagombas and the Bimobas on the other hand, also in the 1990s. In 1999 and 2000, 34 women were killed in cold blood probably for ritual purposes in and around Accra. The causes and perpetrators of these serial killings have still not been found. Perpetual fear grips the whole nation about the safety of women in Accra, the national capital. It is evident that peace seems to elude many African countries.

16

Conditions are no better in the socio-economic fields of developing countries. Food production is very inadequate to feed inhabitants. Governments in almost all developing countries, including Ghana, which have fertile lands, have to rely on food aid from the developed countries. There are refugee camps scattered all over the continent as a result of civil wars. Refugees from Sierra Leone and Liberia live wretched lives in neighbouring Guinea and Ghana. Refugees from Burundi, Rwanda and Congo and from tension-packed areas in Africa spread all over the continent.

While the developed countries are comfortable with small families, the developing countries believe in large families, which they cannot cater for. According to Sarpong (1986), the traditional Ghanaian wife has an average of eight children while the husband may have 15 children. There is poverty, indebtedness and corruption in the developing countries. But corruption becomes visible only when those in power die or are overthrown as were the cases in Nigeria (Abacha), Indonesia (Suharto) or Cote d'Ivoire (Bedie).

CONCLUSION

In conclusion, it can be said that since the eastern bloc collapsed, the tempo of globalization has speeded up at an unprecedented pace. Developing countries, therefore, have access to the world market, technology and information, financial and material support and also international platforms. They have to respond to international demands to liberalize and integrate their trade. They have to promote regional trade and develop democratic institutions.

Globalization has forced countries to adopt fresh ideas of development and participation in the global market. All categories of people are to be given equal opportunities to safeguard their rights and participate in socio-political development. Unfortunately, however, developing countries are handicapped by a myriad of problems and can, therefore, not effectively participate in the global development.

17

The million dollar question now is, what is the future of the developing countries in globalization in the face of these problems? Two of these problems namely, unemployment and rural development are discussed in the next two chapters.

Chapter 2

PROBLEMS OF UNEMPLOYMENT

Introduction

The economies of developing countries like Ghana, are in a more critical situation than those of developed countries. Even those of Côte d'Ivoire and Nigeria, which are relatively viable because of support by large-scale plantations and petrol-chemical industries respectively, cannot be properly managed. These countries cannot provide employment to the majority of their people either. Even, an oil-rich developing country such as Venezuela surprisingly has a high rate of unemployment. Kenya and Tanzania share similar developmental problems with other highly populated countries such as Egypt, Pakistan and India (Harbison 1968). They cannot develop their industries nor can they offer employment opportunities to their people.

However, favoured or not, all developing countries share two crucial developmental problems. These are the inability to solve the problem of unemployment (especially youth unemployment) and how to mobilize the population for effective rural development. We believe that in solving both problems, innovative adult education (especially non-formal education) has a major role to play.

Definition of Unemployment

The *Longman's Dictionary of Contemporary English* defines unemployment as "the condition of lacking a job". In Ghana in 1960, when the population was about 6,727,000 the total labour force in the industrial sector was 879,000 (13%) (1960 Ghana Population Reports). In 1997, the working force in the industrial sector of Ghana was 17 per cent of the labour force while agriculture had 47 percent *(World Development Report 1998/1999)*. Many of those in agriculture were self-employed on their own small farms. They claimed to be employed when, in deed, they could not feed themselves. The modern sector in Ghana cannot employ even a quarter of the unemployed youth. The service sector employs thirty six percent of those employed in the system. The majority of those who qualify to work, the "employables", cannot be employed either in the agricultural, modern, or the service sector.

The employment situation in the developing countries has not improved in the 21st century. The situation in Ghana is illustrated as an example of the employment situation in developing countries. In Ghana, only 14.5 per cent of the economically active population are employees (Ghana Statistical Service 2002). Almost two-thirds (65.7 per cent) of the economically active population claim to be self-employed with no employees working with them. About half (49.2 per cent) of these workers are farmers with small holdings and traders (14.2 per cent) with low capital and turn-over. They work mainly in the informal sector because without basic education their economic opportunities are limited to the informal sector only. They are also unable to tackle poverty more effectively. Their prospects for economic survival depend on market forces and the weather. Some of those who claim to be self-employed work for one, two or three days in a week (Ghana Statistical Service, 2002).

The same report (GSS, Ibid) notes that 11.5 per cent of the economically active citizens are unemployed while 7.3 per cent have jobs but are not working. The implications are that only the minority (14.5 per cent) mentioned above, have regular sources of income while others depend on market forces for their livelihood.

In the view of Blaug (1973) however, unemployment is more than the absence of jobs or the inability to take a job. He explains that the 'employment problem' is primarily a problem of inadequate income and only secondarily one of insufficient work opportunities. To him a person is employed only if one gets adequate income from one's employment to sustain oneself. He then suggests that the ultimate objective of any government policy should not just be to provide more jobs but to provide those jobs that yield enough income to sustain a reasonable standard of living.

The perception of unemployment was first clearly put forward by Callaway (1966). He defines unemployment in terms of the inability of people, including workers of all categories to afford regular 'square meals' during the previous nine months. In Ghana, in 1992, it was reported that 31.4 per cent of the population (34.3 per cent in the rural areas and 26.7 per cent in the urban centres) lived below the poverty line (World Report, 1998/1999). The implications are that almost a third of the population cannot afford regular square meals. Both Blaug and Callaway, therefore, see those engaged in one type of work or the other and those who cannot make ends meet though they may be employed, as unemployed.

Types of Unemployment

Before going into the complexities of the causes of unemployment, we have to note that poverty and its subsequent inability to live above starvation levels are important indicators of unemployment. The majority of workers in developing countries like Ghana, one might say, are unemployed when one considers the definition of unemployment — as a situation where people are faced with inadequate income to meet their needs. In Ghana for instance, graduate teachers and civil servants, who hopefully are in the middle class, cannot make ends meet. Some convert their private cars into taxis and become part-time taxi drivers. Others become farmers but with inadequate knowledge of farming. They invest their inadequate resources in farm projects. In the long run, it is usually found out that neither of these ventures is worth the trouble. The taxis break down and remain packed at the mechanics' shop with no money to rehabilitate them and the farms also get choked with weeds and not much can be harvested from them.

There are large numbers of people in the working class who cannot make ends meet because of the inadequate remuneration system. Although the International Labour Organization Convention 131 has laid down some conditions for the fixing of daily minimum wage of a worker and fixed it at one dollar, the minimum wage of a Ghanaian worker was ¢2.900 as at August, 2000. (The exchange rate of the dollar was ¢8,500). In 2002, "The take home pay" of the Ghanaian worker hardly takes him home at the end of the month. In the first week of the month, workers have no money left in their pockets or in their bank accounts. One should then understand why the brain drain from Ghana started in the late 1970s: when people began to look for greener pastures to avoid financial embarrassment.

Under-employment

Among workers considered by Blaug (1973) as unemployed are those who cannot afford the luxury of unemployment, and therefore, accept to work for short periods on a part-time basis. Some even accept to work one or two hours. Wages received from such engagements, however, cannot help them live adequately. If anything, it can only help them 'tick' for a while. They are, therefore, only temporarily employed or underemployed.

The other category of the underemployed are those who do no productive work or do little work although they are on the pay rolls of organizations. They include the many messengers, who are absorbed into offices with little work to do. Some of them only move files from one desk to another. Others go to the post offices daily to collect mails but, often, return with no letters. Some people are also employed as drivers in offices where there are no vehicles to drive.

The phenomenon of underemployment is a common feature in developing countries and especially in the agricultural sector. Many people in developing countries claim they are farmers. Although, they may have the potential to work, they lack the capital to buy farm inputs or the necessary machinery to be used to supplement labour efforts. Thus, the total production per man-acre in the developing world is sorrowfully low as compared to what prevails in developed countries.

Seasonal unemployment

Seasonal unemployment is also very common in developing countries. People are employed to work on farms during the peak cocoa or maize season and in industries towards the Christmas season to meet production targets and satisfy seasonal demands. At the end of the season, they are declared redundant.

Disguised unemployment

Another variant of the unemployment situation is disguised unemployment. This is commonly found among farming communities. In most African countries, a plural system of land tenure is maintained. Access to land may be through inheritance, marriage, sharecropping or renting, buying or begging. It may also be acquired as a gift. Land shortage, however, occurs only in isolated enclaves in Ghana. It is not widespread. Large families work on the same piece of land because of lack of adequate farmland. As a result of the unfavourable land tenure system in Ghana, for instance, some families have to work on the same patch of land as the years roll by. Production margins, therefore, drop yearly as the fertility of the land decreases. Even some adult members of the family do not have their own farms although they claim to be farmers. The problem of disguised unemployment is compounded by the increasingly large family sizes. Large families have to work on small family lands, using traditional methods of food production. This is the case in some parts of the Upper East Region of Ghana where large families till small arid farmlands each farming season.

Structural unemployment

Structural unemployment occurs when there is a sudden change in the demand for one product in favour of another. This may also be due to the lucrative nature of one job as compared to the other. In Ghana, some people now prefer to work in illegal gold mines, "galamsey" which is more lucrative than farming. This involves geographical mobility with its attendant problems. In some cases, specialists in declining industries like the Asutsuare Sugar Factory and Kade Match Factory, for example, become frustrated and become labourers and watchmen in the emerging textile factories like Akosombo and Juapong Textile Factories.

Voluntary unemployment

The problem of voluntary unemployment also exists. In this case, some people refuse to take up jobs even though they can get them. This is common among housewives. They prefer to stay at home, for personal reasons.

Another group is made up of graduates of the school system who now become very selective in job-seeking. They prefer to look for jobs which are foreign-based or available in private industries that they term as lucrative.

Involuntary unemployment

Among the underemployed are also those who are forced by circumstances to engage in petty trade, primitive crafts, prostitution, begging or carrying luggage at train stations, the ports and lorry parks. Such occupations in the urban centres can hardly give them the earning power to afford a square meal a day. Acquiring their own decent shelter, modern communication gadgets and means of transport seems a far-fetched venture for them. On the whole, however, many African countries are faced with mass involuntary employment.

Causes of Unemployment

Population Explosion
One might attribute the causes of mass unemployment to population explosion which in turn is caused by improvement in health services. Improvement in health services has helped to reduce infant mortality in Ghana from 81 per 1000 in 1994 to 56 per 1000 by the year 2000. The number of nurses increased from 11,200 in 1990 and is projected to reach 28,800 by 2020 (Population Ref. Bureau, 1999). Improvement in health services improves the fertility rate and increases the life expectancy of adults. Life expectancy has increased tremendously because of primary health care programmes, education, medical care and science. In Ghana, the life expectancy of the individual in 1970 was 45. Now it stands at 57 for males and 61 for females (*World Development Report, 1998/1999*). Many more people now therefore spend about a quarter of their lives as children and three quarters as adults. Consequently, many more continue to stay employed longer. New hands cannot be easily employed when the old ones still maintain their positions.

Life in an African society is full of cultural activities. Some of these activities signify important landmarks in the lives of individuals. One such very important activity is the puberty ceremony. Although this ceremony varies from community to community, the principle and objectives are the same. Puberty rites mark the transition from adolescence to adulthood.

Among communities such as the Ibo and Nupe of Nigeria, the Sande and Mende in the Sierra Leone, the Ewe and Krobo in Ghana for example, the idea is to prepare boys for the continuous struggle and endurance which face a man. Boys are taken through drills, occupational training like farming, weaving and hunting and community and family responsibilities. Girls are also confined at home and learn home management and mother craft. These rites initiate individuals into adulthood. Some of these ceremonies end up in weddings or marriages. Pregnancies never preceded these ceremonies. Marriages are also contracted between families only after their sons and daughters are initiated into adulthood. These practices control pregnancies and early marriages. A pregnancy or even immoral behaviour on the part of the youth is frowned upon by society. It is a great source of disgrace to the families involved; but now the situation has changed in the name of modernity. Puberty rites are no longer enforced. The youth meet and contract their own marriages whenever and wherever they meet. In some cases, there are no proper marriages; the couples just agree to live together. The net effect of the marginalization of these rites is the uncontrollable growth in population. Consequently, more people have to join the already saturated labour market.

Again, the proliferation of video and film shows, beauty contests, dancing competitions, concerts, festivals, youth meetings and funerals which have now become more fashionable than before, bring both sexes from different tribes and areas together. At such functions women appear in their best clothes and in their numbers. Love at first sight at these functions results in early marriages and pregnancies. Population control is difficult under these conditions when the open-market approach to marriage is adopted.

25

Use of Capital

The inability of developing countries to accumulate capital, which is a necessary element in economic development, undermines the establishment of industries which could absorb the labour force. Much of the income generated by the developing countries is used to service huge debts and for expansion of social services. In Ghana, despite the efforts being made to service public debt, in the 1999 fiscal year the debt stood at 6,001.25 million dollars. This was about 1.35 per cent increase over that of the previous year. The domestic debt situation is more alarming. The domestic debt has increased at a faster rate from ¢4,495.50 million to ¢5,797.28 million. It recorded a rise of 28.96 per cent (Bank of Ghana 1999).

The government continues to borrow heavily from the commercial banks. It is therefore doubtful if the government could realize its objectives of turning the country into a middle-income nation by 2020 in the face of extensive borrowing and debt servicing. The problem now is how to generate funds to service the debts when the prices of cocoa and gold, the main export earners are falling. Between January and December 1999, the price of cocoa fell by 40 percent while the fuel price increased in the same period by 100 percent (ISSER 2000).

While government revenues increased by an annual average of 1.3 per cent of Gross Domestic Product (GDP) between 1982 and 1989, the increase was only 0.31 per cent of GDP between 1990 and 1999. In 1999, however, government expenditure increased substantially. The expenditure on economic services increased from 10.96 per cent to 21.2 per cent. Also expenditure on general services, community and social services increased over 3 per cent. Thus, the expenditure of government exceeded her income. Government budget in 1999 exceeded the original budget estimates by 1.3 per cent of GDP. Even then huge sums of money could not be paid to contractors who completed their contracts (ISSER, 2000).

The situation discussed above is not peculiar to Ghana. It is a common feature in developing countries. In the face of these difficulties, many governments then attempted to restructure their economies to improve production. As a result of Ghana's Economic Recovery

Programme which started in 1983, there emerged the retrenchment and redeployment exercises. The unemployment situation became worse but was somehow reversed by the divestiture programme, which led to the rehabilitation of some industries and the employment of more hands. The employment level of the divested Tema Steel Company, for example, jumped from 130 to 584 workers within a six-year period (1993/1999). This may be a good example which was also an exception. The employment position has not improved generally. Many developing countries like Ghana can, therefore, not employ the youth.

Moreover, the rich who can help alleviate the unemployment situation are often not interested in investing in the production sector but prefer to invest in the gambling and transport businesses. The gambling business can only temporarily absorb a small part of the labour force. But even then, within a short period, lotto houses are not able to meet their tax obligations and vehicles are not maintained. Many people also prefer to show their wealth and prestige in the purchase and use of the most modern saloon cars rather than investing it in any development programme.

Conditions for the establishment of industries by rich and industrious people are not very favourable. Taxes on industrial concerns are quite high and tax exemptions are not often given to even those in the agricultural sector. Granting of tax exemptions is not a general phenomenon in the Third World. In fact, attractive tax concessions exist only in selective cases. Thus, the employment problem is not tackled by the rich who can establish industries as is expected but have other preferences nor the government, the largest employer, give employment to her citizens.

The School System

The main thesis of Blaug (1973) like that of the "Deschoolers" such as Illich (1972) and Reimer (1972) is that the formal school system is the main factor contributing to the rising rate of youth unemployment. Many writers like Harbison (1968), and Dore, (1976) also complain against the schools for producing "unemployables".

At independence, developing countries believed that formal education was an essential feature of development. Many countries, including Ghana, Tanzania and Zambia embarked on a large-scale expansion of schools. There was also the policy of fee-free and compulsory education in these countries. The youth were then enrolled in schools in their numbers. In the Gold Coast (now Ghana), when in 1951, internal self-government was achieved, the Accelerated Development Plan for Education was drawn. The Convention People's Party government (CPP) of Dr. Kwame Nkrumah, which won majority seats in the Legislative Assembly, embarked upon a vigorous expansion programme of opening elementary schools. Basic education was universal and given to the majority of the youth. Tuition fees in primary schools were abolished. In 1953, Emergency Training Centres were established to give six week courses to teachers to man the schools. These were mainly middle school leavers.

It became apparent that new secondary schools had to be opened to absorb the product of the elementary school system. In addition to the building of secondary schools by the government, a free-market approach to education was adopted. Citizens who could open schools began to build private schools throughout the country. In 1951, there were 13 Government Assisted Secondary Schools and 49 private secondary schools. In 1960, there were 59 Government Secondary Schools including 16 Ghana Education Trust Fund Schools. The latter were built between 1958 and 1960 under a special programme. These Trust Fund Schools were financed largely *(£2.5m)* by the Ghana Cocoa Marketing Board (Foster,1965).

It was at this juncture that the local administrators, education planners and development strategists could have easily reviewed the transplant of the British curriculum into the Gold Coast to meet the demands of the emerging society. But the British colonial syllabus continued to be used in the schools. For one reason, the school administrators and the politicians were beneficiaries of the British education system and wanted to maintain the status quo. Occupations, like farming, available in the developing countries were not sufficiently catered for by the schools. By the 1970s, some countries including Zambia were still writing London GCE "O" and "A" Level examinations in their schools. The products would only be interested in white-collar jobs, which were not available. A host of problems including unemployment and lack of community participation and improvement was then created by this transplant of the British school system. The problems were compounded when the criterion used to justify the existence of the schools was merely numbers. No serious attempts were made to create job-training opportunities for the people.

From the mid 1980s, Ghana attempted to overhaul its educational system to respond to national and international demands. This resulted in the introduction of the JSS/SSS concept. Since 1987 when the Government of Ghana introduced the JSS/SSS system of education, the unemployment problem has rather worsened. The idea was to place emphasis on vocational and technical courses so that graduates from these schools could come out with technical and vocational skills and establish their own small-scale businesses or become readily employable. But the employment situation has not improved much. There are not enough technical and vocational tutors to teach in the JSS/SSS. Many schools do not have equipped workshops to train prospective artisans. The graduates often find it difficult to acquire tools and equipment to establish their workshops at the end of their studies.

The current enrolment figures and the number of schools built clearly reflect the problems the schools create. Many entrants who cannot proceed to the top of the educational ladder are frustrated.

Table 2.1

Enrolment at the various educational levels:

Level	Number	%
Tertiary	36,629	1.2
Secondary	224,532	7.5
Basic	2,722,494	91.3
Total	2,983,655	100.0

Compiled from GES National Education Forum Report, 1999.

The data in Table 2.1 are not pleasant enough. Over 90 percent of those in the school system in 1999 were at the basic level. Less than two per cent were at the tertiary level. The casualty level at all stages is not encouraging. The sad issue is that not much attention is paid to the school casualties in the provision of alternate institutions to cater for them.

Table 2.2

Number of schools at the various levels from the basic to the highest

Level	Number	YEAR
Basic	18346	1997/98
Secondary	504	1998/98
Tertiary:		
Polytechnics	9	1997/98
Universities (National)	5	1997/98

Compiled from GES National Education Forum Report, 1999.

Table 2.2 explains why the number of students decreases from the lower to the higher levels. The higher the level, the less the vacancies. This trend appears to be the norm in many countries. What then is needed is non-formal education for the majority who fall by the wayside or branch to other areas so that they can always be kept abreast with new developments.

Industrialization

At independence in 1957, Ghana pursued a policy of industrialization to develop and give employment to school leavers. Many industries were then established. But many of these industries which were soon to collapse were built in or near the towns. In the Upper East Region of Ghana there were the Pwalugu Tomato Factory, the Bawku Oil Mills, the Zuarungu Meat Factory which have all collapsed. The youth who moved there only helped to increase the redundant labour force and increase urban problems of over-population, slums and social problems such as prostitution, drug abuse and robbery.

There were large-scale state farms sited in areas, which supported the CPP Government. An example was the state cotton farm established at Abutia in the Volta Region that initially absorbed a large labour force. Today, one can hardly see any signs of the farm at the village. These industries collapsed because of poor maintenace. Marketing of products became a problem and management deficiency was evident. For most cases, also the appropriate surveys were not made nor were their viability tested. While the schools, which were to produce the required manpower to feed these industries were maintained the industries themselves collapsed. Those that survived could not be expanded. Maintenance of the surviving industries was also difficult. They could neither promote rural development nor give job opportunities to the school leavers.

Modernization

Harbison (1968) attributes the main cause of unemployment to modernization. In explaining this position, he differentiates between two types of economies in developing countries: the modern and the traditional. The modern sector in the urban areas is fully within the large-scale world wide monetary economy. But in the face of globalization and competition, many industries in the developing countries cannot survive.

When labour saving machinery is introduced or when profit margins fall, some of those employed are also often declared redundant. Redundancy has thus become a necessary feature but painful exercise in the industrial sector. There exists a tight control over employment. It is, therefore, not surprising that many of the energetic educated youth who even learn some vocations are also considered too young or inexperienced to be employed. At this point, one might refer to adverts in the most widely circulated Ghanaian daily, *the Daily Graphic*. There

31

were ten adverts *in the Daily Graphic* No. 147989 of August 18, 2000. All the adverts, for instance, had almost disqualified young school leavers and new university graduates from applying. Seven of these adverts are briefly discussed.

SALESMEN:
Experienced Salesmen with not less than 5 years experience in the drinks distributive trade are required to fill vacant places.

Qualification: SSSCE, GCE 'O' Level or GCE 'A' Level with five (5) credits including English and Mathematics. A Diploma in Marketing from any recognized institution will be an advantage.

This advert was in the 18th August 2000 issue but the closing date for application was 20th August 2000. Only two days are allowed for the receipt of applications. The application was to be made through the most unreliable electronic media in a developing country such as Ghana.

Vanef/State Transport Company
Recruitment of Drivers:
Applicants must possess GCE Ordinary Level, Technical Certificate or equivalent and Professional Certificate (License "A").

Experience:
Five (5) years or more experience in driving a heavy duty bus.

ADVERT NO. 182
We are part of a Transnational group across West Africa with offices in London and USA, and are holding leading shares in food and beverage segments. To further the growth and expansion plans in Ghana we seek candidates for the following positions:

Accounts Executive: Age 35-40 years
Qualification: Degree in Accounting or RSA III or its equivalent
Experience: Minimum of 5 years.

ADVERT 183

Personnel and Administrative Manager, Age 40–45 years
Qualification: Degree in Sociology or Public Administration
Experience: Minimum 10 years

ADVERT NO. 184

Wanted "experienced drivers" capable of working late in the evening. The applicants should not be more than 30 years with a minimum driving experience of 5 years. He is to be a holder of SSS or GCE Certificate.

CARE INTERNATIONAL

Reproductive Health Adviser
Qualification and Experience
A degree in Public Health Nursing or similar qualification
Several years' practical experience in the reproductive
— Health field,
— Strong training experience,
— Strong written and oral communication skills,
— Computer literacy.

It can be deduced from these advertisements that, many school leavers and graduates of the Universities are eliminated from applying for jobs because they have not had long working experience with reputable or recognized organizations. The age qualifications are also high and disqualify the young school leavers.

Attitude of Guardians and School Leavers

The increase in the number of the educated unemployed youth is also due to the attitude of parents, guardians and the school leavers themselves. According to parents and guardians, they have sent their wards to school with the hope of getting them out of farming. It is the pride of parents and members of the extended family, if their wards are employed in offices in cities. An investment in their wards' education is an investment for a better life and a decent job for the family in the city.

A visit to the son, daughter or a relative working in the capital is a source of pride for the parents. In a similar vein, a visit of the son from the urban centre in decent attire and more especially in a car is a source of pride to both the son and the parents. Many parents, therefore, encourage their wards to move to the urban areas, for white-collar jobs. The youth, therefore, converge into the cities where there are not enough jobs for them. The traditional social system, which caters for them in the rural setting, is not available in the urban centres. The unemployed in these centres, therefore, face much difficulty, yet they continue to live in the cities.

The benefits attached to white-collar jobs also attract people to the cities. Some of these benefits include prestige, riding in one's car or company's car, sickness benefits, leave, maternity and leave allowances, use of workers' canteen, guarantee of one's monthly salary and handsome end-of-service benefits "the golden handshake" as some people term it.

Some workers in the modern sector attend local and international conferences. There is much prestige and respect attached to travelling abroad. The coveted title given to people in West Africa who travel abroad is "been to". Everybody would like his ward or he himself to get this coveted title of "a been to". Many people, therefore, leave work on the farms and village industries in search of white –collar jobs in towns.

CONSEQUENCES OF UNEMPLOYMENT

The modern sector attracts the unemployed to move to the urban areas to try their luck. The unemployed youth are thus found all over the cities in Africa. Harbison (1968) illustrates that in Ibadan, Nigeria, out of an unemployed labour force of 30,000, more than 20,000 were recent school products. This situation is not limited to Nigeria alone. There exists widespread unemployment among the educated youth all over the urban areas of the twelve Anglophone countries in Africa namely,

Gambia, Ghana, Kenya, Lesotho, Malawi, Nigeria, Sierra Leone, Swaziland, Tanzania, Uganda and Zambia when Harbison conducted a survey in these countries. The situation has worsened since then.

The size of the labour reserve army increases yearly. Battalions of the army engage themselves in selling handkerchiefs, dog chains, chocolates among others, along busy streets. Others sell newspapers, toilet rolls, car dusters, shaving blades, and shoe polish. All these wayside traders are seen at T-junctions and near traffic lights in cities such as Accra and Lagos. They keep on chasing passengers in moving vehicles. No one knows the distance they run daily. This exercise continues whether "rain or shine". Others keep on roaming about the cities looking for non-existent jobs.

Many of the youth go to the towns to make some money at all costs. Some of the girls are seen sitting in hair salons and at social centres to while away time. As a result of this desperate situation in which they find themselves, some engage themselves in some social vices like highway and armed robbery, murder of fellow men and women for ritual purposes, drug abuse, alcoholism as well as prostitution which ultimately leads to the spread of HIV/AIDS.

Yet, others come to the offices of the Institute of Adult Education to register for Senior Secondary School courses to better their grades. Some can not pay their registration fees duly but do so at their own pace when they gather funds. In some cases, they have to withdraw because they cannot afford the payment. Some find the afternoon non-residential programme cumbersome.

Many of the unemployed prefer to stay in the towns, live under difficult and pitiful conditions and endure hardships such as hunger and starvation. They may stay with relatives, friends or people from their communities whom they might not have known earlier on. Some even sleep at the entrance of shops and offices and on verandas of houses. They have to keep on roaming about or stay with friends in town till late in the evening when the verandas are free for their use. The majority of them do not have any permanent address nor do they have any decent places to sleep other than under trees, at lorry parks, train stations and in market stalls. It is a pathetic scene.

As the energetic youth leave the traditional agricultural sector, production in this sector decreases drastically while unemployment rises sharply in the urban setting. The people who are to be trained to participate in national and the global economic process have been trapped in a vicious cycle of unemployment.

SUGGESTED SOLUTIONS

Many writers including Blaug (1973) made some suggestions for arresting the rising problems of unemployment. Blaug suggests

1   that the school curriculum should be reformed;
2   examinations should be abolished;
3   secondary schools must be vocationalized;
4   enrolment must be controlled;
5   school fees should be increased to reduce intake and
6   that functional literacy programmes and drop-out of school training programmes must be introduced.

Many of these suggestions are, however, long term programmes and some may even increase the unemployment rate in the long run. Increase in school fees will tend to frustrate parents who can not afford to pay high school fees. Their wards will then, be withdrawn from the schools and school drop-out rate will rise. The abolition of examinations, the control of enrolment and reduction in the intake will promote illiteracy in the country.

The author holds the view that even if the curriculum is reformed to equip school leavers with skills, non-formal education is necessary to keep up the interest of workers in their vocations. Mobilization is required from non-formal education organizations to train and keep people in jobs in the rural areas. The role of non-formal organizations in keeping the youth in their vocations is thus emphasized. Any attempt to call the youth to the land without the appropriate education and attractions, as it happened in the early 1970s in Ghana, will fail. Any attempt to remove the benefits attached to the modern sector or to remove the attractions as has been suggested by some people will always be resisted by workers. Any effort to induce some industries to employ more hands will be a failure because the raw materials are unavailable. Employers will protest seriously since profit margins would be reduced. One of the best ways to solve the employment problem is to mobilize the reserve labour force through non-formal education and engage them in some more productive work such as agricultural and artisanship, towards rural, national and global development.

Although politicians may deny the existence of unemployment, it exists as a very painful social problem. It denies the individual the dignity of labour and undermines his social status. Such a person cannot practise skills and experiences acquired in school and society and is demoralized. He suffers from psychological problems like depression and frustration. The victim may be tempted to engage in vices mentioned earlier on.

The unemployment issue is a very crucial one. It is not just a matter of providing jobs that generate enough income to sustain an improved standard of living. It includes workers of all categories who can not afford regular square meals for three months. It affects the lives of many people in the developing countries because of the extended family system. The problem is also a global concern.

Chapter 3

PROBLEMS OF RURAL DEVELOPMENT

INTRODUCTION

One of the major concerns of the Doomsters School of Thought is that globalization will widen the development gap between the developed and developing countries because of the problems facing the development process in the latter. It indicates that globalization is nothing but imperialism. For developing countries to develop fully in this era of globalization, rural development must be given the necessary push and attention.

In this chapter, therefore, the concept of community participation and improvement is defined. Various factors retarding the progress of rural and national development towards globalization have been identified and some strategies adopted by some governments towards this process have been illustrated.

Causes of Low Community Participation and Rural Improvement

Community participation and improvement in rural areas here refer to all attempts made by people themselves and at times in collaboration with government departments and other agencies to embark upon projects to improve upon their conditions and the environment. It could be in the form of construction of roads, community centres, street drains, school building, water works and health centres. It could also be street cleaning as well as engaging in agricultural projects. There are many factors leading to the underdevelopment of the rural areas in developing countries. Some of these are discussed below.

The Urban Dilemma

At independence, many developing countries attempted to develop their communities by embarking first upon large-scale industrialization programmes. Many of the development activities were centred close to cities and many collapsed as mentioned earlier on. Yet the trend of migration to the cities continues. According to Asamoa (2001) ten million rural people, on the average, migrate to urban centres in Africa yearly.

Inhabitants of modern cities like Ouagadougou, Tema, Accra, Lome, Lagos, Dar-es-Salaam and Gaborone, continue to benefit from many kinds of social services. There are, in these cities, comparatively cheap goods, entertainment, health-care delivery services, pipe-borne water, better and higher educational opportunities. There are also good roads, electricity, hotels and restaurants, and all those things that go into making life modern and enjoyable. One issue then seemed to be certain — a mass exodus of rural dwellers into the cities became the trend. Much emphasis had been placed on the development of large-scale physical projects. Immediately before and during the 1960s, this was the trend of development programmes in all developing countries.

One would have thought that the under-development inherited at independence by the developing countries would have been solved sooner or later due to the initial enthusiasm for development in all fields of activity; that a wider support for these programmes would follow especially, in the rural areas. A strong foundation for national and international development could have been laid from the rural level where the majority of the people live. As it was observed, however, the enthusiasm faded away for many reasons.

The Failure of the Bureaucratic Approach to Community Improvement

The most obvious reason was that plans and projects conceived in the cities did not necessarily lead to successful rural development. The top-down planning approach to development may fail to produce the expected results when communities are not taken as partners in the process. People become disillusioned about the implementation of these programmes whose objectives they are not very clear about. At times, they are suspicious of the motives of the administrators of these programmes. It is very necessary to get people or at least their leaders involved in the planning of development programmes so that they can have some pride in identifying themselves with the programmes. Community entry techniques such as baseline studies, group discussions and especially, focus group discussions and transect walks could be organized to solicit information on the development needs of the people. They would then understand the need for such programmes. Thus, the initial development projects were misconceived in the first place. The argument advanced here, however, is not that community participation is a decisive factor in development. It is a necessary element in the development process.

The Government as "Father Christmas"

There are other problems, which retard development. There is the view that the government is "Father Christmas". Many people look up to central government as the giant development agent that should provide all the developmental needs of people. This position is due to the very fact that during political electioneering campaigns and after governments have been voted into power, politicians and members of government make many vain promises towards community and national development. In the event of military coups, the same promises are made by the soldiers. People, therefore, expect governments to honour their promises and develop the communities.

Chieftaincy

Chieftaincy is an institution which includes the chief, his council of elders and his regalia. The chief, the central figure in the chieftaincy institution, is described as "a person who, hailing from the appropriate royal family and lineage, has been validly nominated, elected or selected and enstooled, enskinned or installed as a chief or Queenmother in accordance with the relevant customary law and usage" (Republic of Ghana 1992: 168). The chief is not thus an ordinary citizen but a royal who is customarily installed as a chief and is expected to be the central figure in community and rural development efforts.

In pre-colonial Africa, the chief wielded executive political, social and economic powers in his chiefdom. The colonialists, realizing the useful roles played by the chief in community development, maintained chieftaincy but reduced its powers. Although chieftaincy has gone through many changes since colonial days its contribution in the field of non-formal education and development is still valid in the modern era. By and large, it is a tool for non-formal education. Since independence, therefore, African governments have restored a large measure of administrative and community development powers to chiefs. In Ghana, for example, the 1992 Republic Constitution restores the position of chiefs when it states: " the institution of chieftaincy together with its traditional councils as established by customary law and usage, is hereby guaranteed" (Republic of Ghana 1992: 164).

The position of the chief as the religious leader of his people is of paramount importance in the education and development process. The traditional belief is that the chief is the embodiment of the dead, those alive and those yet unborn. He is the embodiment of the culture of the people. Many Africans, therefore, respect the chief's authority more than that of politicians. They believe in the potency of traditional religious beliefs and practices symbolized by the chief, to solve their problems. As Mbiti (1977:1) explains

> Wherever the African is, there is his religion: he carries it to the fields where he is sowing seeds or harvesting a new crop; he takes it with him to the beer party or to attend a funeral; and if he is educated, he takes religion with him to the examination room at school or in the University; if he is a politician, he takes it to the House of Parliament.

The scenario above may have been exaggerated. The implications, however, are that the African, in many things, is religious. He, therefore, looks up to the chief, the religious leader, for protection, fertility of his crops, success of his business and life, maintenance of peace and more importantly, for the promotion of development. Thus the chief initiates programmes and projects and performs rites to advance the general welfare and prosperity of his people and community. He is a symbol of community education and development, and a facilitator of the non-formal education process.

The prevalence of peace is a necessary condition for the promotion of education and development. A laudable traditional primary duty of a chief is the maintenance of peace in the community. By tradition, the chief is a law-maker, administrator and war leader. As a peace-maker, the chief settles disputes among his subjects and unites them. He organizes search parties to arrest criminals who are brought to book. He maintains law and order in the community.

As the commander of his army, he is the only person who can declare war and participate in it when the security of his state is threatened. He is the only person to stop the war on the advice of his elders. As an administrator, he assigns duties to sub-chiefs and title holders. He designs checks and balances to control the excessive power of clan chiefs and elders to prepare the ground for education and development to progress.

The chief is an economic planner in the community. He is the custodian of land, the most valuable resource, which he holds in trust for his subjects. He protects it from being indiscriminately sold, exploited, degraded, polluted or burnt. He leases it in consultation with land owners, to individuals and organizations for development projects. He is also expected to own stool land which is developed to illustrate his economic standing and inspire hard work among the youth. Briefly put, he is responsible for land conservation and development and environmental sanitation. As an economic adviser, the chief encourages families and citizens to take to one trade or the other. This is one reason why festivals and cultural activities are organized for people to showcase their handicrafts, crops and wealth. Subjects in business are encouraged to continue to perform creditably while the unemployed are advised to learn a trade.

The chief serves as a public relations officer linking the community to central government, district assemblies and all types of non-governmental organizations. He draws the attention of these institutions to the developmental needs of his people and solicits support for them. The chief and especially, the queenmother provide guidance and counselling services to the youth on marriage and vocational matters. Both receive and host state and private visitors and monitor their activities and movement in the interest of rural development.

The chief is concerned with the mobilization of the community for the planning of local development activities and especially, communal labour. He raises funds for these development projects and participates actively in and monitors the progress of these self-help projects such as the construction of school buildings and markets.

The educational role played by the chief in community development is also very significant. The chief collaborates with institutions such as the Ministry of Health to carry out educational campaigns on sanitation, HIV/AIDS and immunization against diseases. He works in close collaboration with the Ministry of Education to mobilize people to participate in functional literacy programmes. Since the chief commands a lot of respect in his locality and speaks the same language as his people, the chances are that people listen to him and take the programmes seriously. The chief's position, as a traditional leader and facilitator in the non-formal education process, has enhanced the maintenance of peace and the development of rural economies. On the whole, chieftaincy is a model for cultural identity and a tool for non-formal education and rural development.

Chieftaincy, which could be the mobilizing force for rural development appears to be just a ceremonial institution now. In the traditional African society chieftaincy has been a potential force in community education and improvement. Chiefs could mobilize people to work on any project after the necessary consultations with their elders have been made. But this is traditional rather than modern democracy, whereby the town crier summons the people to discuss and plan community projects. It might be projects on health, social or economic development. The town crier just passes the message on to the people who respond by coming together to solve the problems or participate in community development activities. As a result of the important roles chiefs play in rural development, they are not allowed by tradition to live outside their homes. Chiefs are expected to stay with their subjects and provide the leadership necessary for community education, skill training and development.

However, these are no longer entirely realities. Many chiefs, including paramount chiefs, now, stay and work in urban centres and only pay visits to their traditional areas on weekends. The chief needs to be gainfully employed to be able to perform his functions.

Some chiefs have become political party functionaries while some have taken party political appointments contrary to the provisions of the 1992 Ghana Constitution. These chiefs stand on political platforms, sing and dance to political songs of their political parties. They are engaged in propaganda rather than in education and reality which chieftaincy stands for. Party symbols mean more to them than their regalia, traditional emblems and attire. Mobilization of the people for development programmes has ceased to be the priority function of some chiefs in Ghana.

There are other factors, which have weakened the position of chiefs as development agents. One of these factors is the emergence of the modern administrators and the tension between these administrators and some chiefs. Another common factor here is the inhibiting effect of political power struggle, in this case between the chiefs and the new politically appointed administrators. When the People's Defence Committees (PDCs) for example were established in Ghana in the early 1980s, tension developed between some chiefs and members of these newly created political institutions. This conflict is one of the reasons for the apathy in the attendance of public meetings and in participation in development projects by those who support the chiefs. Many of the chiefs in the rural areas are illiterate or have low formal education background. They are not able either to mobilize the dynamic youth or liaise with NGOs and government departments to undertake rural development activities. This is another reason for emphasizing the need to foster educational groups at the local level. They can be neutral groups for community improvement programmes.

Despondency

Lack of enthusiasm for participating in development programmes is also due to the fact that the rural folk, like their urban counterparts, are subjected to the payment of different kinds of taxes including poll, income and property taxes and levies on utility services. The notion is that the government would supplement such taxes collected to develop the various communities. Moreover, the country's natural resources and foreign exchange earners like minerals, timber and cocoa come from the rural areas. Foodstuffs from the rural areas feed the urban dwellers and administrators. The rural people are not happy that incomes generated in the rural areas are not used to develop their areas but the urban centres. In view of these complaints, many people especially those in the rural areas, are despondent of joining voluntary associations and taking part in rural development projects. If rural dwellers pay taxes and work to feed urban dwellers they deserve a share of national resources.

The Notion that the Rural Folks Cannot Develop Themselves

Some urban dwellers and administrators have the wrong notion that rural folks, given the resources and motivation, cannot develop their environment; that they are used to their poor conditions and inadequate facilities and that only large scale governmental projects and massive foreign aid can ginger them to take action. No serious efforts were thus made to support rural development. The fact however, remains that given the relevant education and motivation, rural people can make vital contributions towards community and national development.

Illiteracy

Illiteracy is widespread in developing countries. In 1995, the literacy rate for males and females in Africa was 66 percent and 46 percent respectively (Population Reference Bureau 1995). The illiteracy situation is worse in rural areas than in the urban areas. Some rural Africans in the 21st century still determine the time by the crowing of the cock at dawn and by the location of the sun during the day. According to Freire (1985), many illiterate rural people only exist in the world. They are surrounded by myths, which limit their sense of initiative. Almost all

45

their actions are controlled by traditional beliefs. They give magical explanation to every event and find it difficult to differentiate between propaganda and education. Thus, they are easily manipulated by those in power who always promise them the moon. Their interest centres on biological needs like food and when these needs are met they are satisfied. They are closely attached to cultural activities and festivals and are afraid of change. Illiteracy limits their world to their environment.

Illiteracy has denied people the opportunity to actively participate in the political issues of their country. Politicians fight for power and wealth, playing on the ignorance of the illiterate electorate. Petty gifts and wild promises mean so much to them and determine the trend of voting among the electorate. It is a pathetic scenario in this age of globalization when people can not initiate and participate in development programmes.

Some may argue that lack of capital has accounted for lack of participation in community improvement in the rural areas. But capital invested in development will not produce the desired results unless the problem of the high incidence of illiteracy is tackled. Appropriate non-formal education must be organized alongside any development programme. Dore (1976:1) explains the importance of education to eliminate illiteracy as a necessary component, in the developing process when he noted that,

> Capital given to Europe under the Marshall plan, capital given to Japan to restore its devastated industries, proved productive because those countries had people with the knowledge necessary to make it productive

He went on to contrast this situation with the lack of adequate education in the developing countries by stating that:

> Similar investment in Indonesia or Burma, which lacked engineers and managers and technicians of the richer countries failed to produce the same result. And so economists discovered — or actually rediscovered because Adam Smith had never overlooked the point — the importance of complementary human factors, factors of investment in human resources (Dore 1976:1).

The major human problem has already been noted. It is a question of education, motivation and mobilization. A more practical approach to involving the people in functional literacy programmes to work at their local levels and to respond to the imperatives of globalization will reduce the rate of unemployment and contribute to rural development. It will also reduce poverty and other social problems. Development will start when the majority of people are engaged in one form of functional education activity or the other. The importance of education in community, national and global development was clearly demonstrated when in the 19th century the educated mid-level personnel in Europe started the industrial revolution. Planners of education must, therefore, link educational programmes especially non-formal educational programmes to both rural development and community participation in development projects.

Socio-political Problems

There are some serious social problems which undermine the development process. One of these is the breakdown of the traditional family system which until recently was a strong basic unifying development factor. Now, family members do not readily accept family roles and responsibilities and are not affected by sanctions. Schools and social groups rather than families have become the transmitters of values.

The traditional forms of relationships based on the bonds of the nuclear family and the extended family are in crisis. The traditional family ceases to provide services it used to provide to its members. It is no longer able to provide shelter, communal meals and security from the storms of life. When one is in financial crisis, or in some difficult conditions one is hardly supported by family members but by his employers, banks, or social groups. The extended family system is fast collapsing and individuals have become restless in their own environment.

The menace of Acquired Immune Deficiency Syndrome (AIDS), the increased crime wave, drug abuse, perennial teenage pregnancy, chronic poverty and unbearable environmental degradation have become big global problems threatening the lives of rural communities and retarding the progress of development. Non-formal education has

47

become imperative for the management of resources and facilities and for solving social problems if globalization must be meaningful. Legislation and advertisements on the consequences of these social problems will not solve them. What is necessary is the constant organization of non-formal education programmes to sufficiently draw the attention of people to these hazards.

A more serious problem which undermines the development process in Africa is the intervention of the military in the political administration of countries. Baynham (1986) explained that in the first 25 years (1957 – 1982) of independent black Africa, almost half of the states were governed by their armies as a result of military coups d'etat. He continued to explain that by the end of 1984, there were 84 successful and seven abortive coups in black Africa with their attendant problems. Baynham (1986) intimated that military intervention brought the clock of modernization and industrialization in Africa backwards. Some of the effects of the intervention mentioned by him include the following:

> Military intervention brought into Africa instability and regular turnover of regimes. Between 1966 and 1977 there were seven attempted coups in Congo Brazzaville while between 1966 and 1982 seven military regimes ruled Ghana. Each military regime or attempted coup brought instability and retarded the progress of African development.

He pointed out that some of the military regimes became corrupt and did ot promote the economic development of their countries. In Guinea and Burkina Faso, nepotism and accumulation of wealth began the very day the soldiers took office. Some of the military leaders like Idi Amin of Uganda and Sani Abacha of Nigeria had simplistic views of economic management and messed up the economic systems of their countries. Baynham continued to comment on the stewardship of military regimes. He complained that some of the military administrators usually increased military expenditures to ensure security. These expenditures impacted negatively upon national economies of countries such as Liberia, Ghana, Uganda and Zaire.

Another serious setback to industrialization brought by the military was the creation of ethnic rivalry, regional conflicts and fratricidal clashes.

These are created by Samuel Doe (Liberia) Idi Amin (Uganda), Kountche (Niger), Thomas Sankara (Burkina Faso) Sese Sekou Mobutu (Zaire) and Gnassingbe Eyadema (Togo).

Almost all the military regimes ruled with decrees and were dictatorial. They undermined democratic principles and scared away investors. In Ghana, soldiers looted the stores of foreigners and especially those of Lebanese and Syrians and forced them out of the country. The soldiers were indisciplined, drunk, and took revenge on their seniors whom they executed. Development could not strive in indisciplined society. The development process, therefore, slowed down in the wake of military adventurism.

In brief, military intervention led to the collapse of the economy of some countries, created conflict situations in others and messed up political systems. In fact, military adventurism has become a problem for all African countries.

Frequent changes of governments in the developing countries have rendered the illiterate electorate powerless and frustrated. Citizens come into contact with new structures, new social classes, new values, new rulers, and new ideologies. In Ghana, a new class of administrators and a new system of political structures like unit committees at the grassroots level have emerged. Illiterate people are, therefore, required to take part in the community decision-making process. In this regard , the non-formal educator is called upon to prepare people to adjust to the changes.

Information Communication Technology (ICT) has turned the world into a global village. The media in its various forms like computers, e-mail, mobile phones, the internet, fax, television and newspapers have engaged the attention of many people in world affairs. The British Broadcasting Corporation (BBC), the Voice of America (VOA), the Cable News Network in America (CNN) and other well known broadcasting houses broadcast news items to the entire world instantly. Wars, ethnic conflicts, plane crashes, football matches and elections in any country have become everybody's concern. Yet, capacities of people in the developing world are not developed to interpret these world events and draw lessons for their sustenance.

Structural Weakness in Developing Economies

The colonial economy was designed to benefit the colonial masters at the expense of African colonies. Unilateral economic decisions taken in the metropolitan countries led to the exploitation of resources from, and reservation of markets in the colonies for the colonial masters. No attempts were made by the colonialists to establish heavy industries in the colonies where the resources were exploited. They developed an appropriate communication system to the resource areas to facilitate the transportation of raw materials to the metropolitan industries and finished products to the colonies. In French West Africa, the harbour in Dakar was developed to serve Senegal, Mauritania and Sudan. The port developed in Abidjan served Côte d'Ivoire and Mali. The Coutonou harbour served Benin and Niger. Coffee and Cocoa plantations were developed in Côte d'Ivoire while banana cultivation was promoted in Guinea. All crops were transported through these ports to feed metropolitan industries.

In British West Africa, similar trends in rail, road, and harbour construction and cash crop cultivation developed. The Takoradi harbour was developed and linked to the mining and cocoa growing areas between 1898 and 1923. By 1927, the gold, bauxite, diamond, cocoa and timber producing areas were within reach of the railway lines in the Gold Coast. Production and exportation of cocoa and palm oil in Nigeria, kolanuts in the Sierra Leone and groundnuts in the Gambia were given a great boost. Food crop production was, however, neglected and left in the hands of the colonies. Colonial policies undermined the development of indigenous small and medium scale industrial sectors and agriculture. Skills in artisanship and craftsmanship disappeared with generations. People in these trades became jobless, poor and miserable. They could not join any co-operatives since colonialists did not encourage the formation of co-operatives. Asamoa (2001) explains that in place of heavy industries the colonialists established light industries for the manufacturing of building materials, repairing and renewal of tyres, printing, book-binding and ceramics. African manufacturers were involved in these light industries which were established in the urban areas.

At independence in the 1960s, however, African leaders like Kwame Nkrumah believed firmly that Africa could easily transplant Western model of industrialization to take Africa on the royal path of industrialization into the millennium. This notion became a fatal one for the development of the continent. Conditions in the continent were not favourable to enhance the growth and development of this transplant. It must be noted that industrialization is an evolutionary process. The industrialization of Europe has been a long process. Certain structures need to be put in place for industrialization to succeed. These include markets and widespread communication systems as developed in Europe. In Europe also, the educational system is well structured producing a variety of cores of skilled workers and professionals. Political stability exists and good industrial management practices are instituted.

In Africa, however, poor trade links among countries exist and the communication systems are deplorable. There is widespread political instability. The farmer is uneducated and poor. No form of end-of-service benefits or health insurance supports him. He hardly gets access to credit facilities and has not developed strong co-operative movements to fight for his rights. Briefly put, weaknesses exist in developing economies.

An important strategy to improve conditions is the application of extension and non-formal education to enhance the creativity and improve the occupational skills of the majority. In view of the above, many developing countries have adopted new strategies to involve people in the development process.

NEW TRENDS IN RURAL DEVELOPMENT

As the globalization process picks up gradually, the main ideas about development by the close of the 1960s are that, man, no matter where he lives, must be the centre of development. Development starts with people through education. People must be given the opportunity to develop and use their talents to live and enjoy full life. Taking this position, Adiseshia (in Fordham, 1980) explains that development means a new international order whereby the yawning economic and poverty gap (sickness, hunger, squalor, ignorance) between the rich and the poor would be bridged. He explains further that development means gainful employment, adequate provision of food for the under-nourished children and their mothers: equalization of opportunities of social, economic and political conditions of life between the developed urban and the poor neglected rural areas. Development in this context means all attempts made to solve some of the problems mentioned above in the interest of the poor rural folk. Emphasis here is on the development of rural communities, where these problems are prevalent.

It is evident from the discussions advanced so far that developing countries cannot use Western models of development wholesale to hasten their development process. There is the need to adopt a different model by borrowing ideas and technology from the Western world. This model must derive from the people's cultural realities to advance their potentials for creativity and innovation. This trend will revive and sustain people's interest in agriculture and local trades. It will provide working opportunities for the majority of people who have been unemployed and poor over the years. It is against this background that Schumacher (1973) has recommended the use of intermediate technology by developing countries to promote the development process.

Schumacher (1973:151) describes this development technology as fairly simple, suitable for maintenance and repair on the spot. Workers are more easily trained to handle equipment. It is not capital intensive. Supervision of workers and control of equipment are simple. The majority of items needed by the rural poor such as building materials, clothing, agricultural implements and household utensils are produced by this technology. Appropriate processing and storage facilities are produced so that people will add value to their products and have a good price for them. Central and local governments and non-governmental organisations have to, however, provide technical and credit support.

The use of intermediate technology, Schumacher believes,

introduces an alternative development strategy in developing countries. By this technology, traditional poultry, craft industries, black smithing, soap making and weaving are revived and improved through advanced technology from the West. The majority of the youth can be trained in these economic activities which are people-centred and self-reliant and established in many communities. Schumacher (1973) believes that this process will promote spatial integrations of rural and urban economies within the global system. It will also reduce the rural-urban drift of the youth.

Agriculture, the main occupation of the people, must be tackled as the basis of rural development. In some African countries like Burundi and Burkina Faso where more than 90 percent of the total population live in the rural areas and are engaged in agricultural activities (Coombs and Ahmed 1974), there has to be great emphasis on agricultural development. In this context, many writers like Asamoa (2001) call for a systematic depeasantization of the African rural economy through the use of non-formal education and appropriate intermediate technology strategies. The African farmer must be helped to overcome the problems associated with the cultivation of the old crops such as sisal, cotton, rubber, coffee and cocoa. Appropriate technology practices could also be applied to help the farmer to cultivate new crops such as Indian mango, Brazilian cashew and improved varieties of palm trees, maize and yam. The problems of post harvest losses of crops, poor and inadequate storage facilities and the use of obsolete farming equipment have to be seriously tackled.

The success of agricultural development programmes through non-formal education will have effect on other sectors of the economy. Small scale and cottage industries in carpentry, cloth and basket weaving, pottery, masonry and the handicrafts will be established. Markets will be built to dispose of the goods produced. The problems of unemployment will be reduced and community improvement enhanced. It was in view of these and the failure of earlier attempts at development from the national level that many countries have embarked upon rural development programmes. Rural development has thus become the chief priority and conventional wisdom of many developing countries since the sixties.

In the Gezira Project of the Sudan, for example, the adoption of modern farming techniques, the use of irrigation in farming, the establishment of communication and cottage industries led to improvement in the general living standards of the people. Similar non-formal education programmes were introduced in India, Nepal and the Philippines to get local populations involved in the development process.

Rural development programmes in Ghana have been in existence since the early 1960s. The first was contained in the Seven-Year Development Plan (1963–1964/1969–1970), drawn by the Nkrumah government. The second was the 1969–70 Ghana Youth and Rural Development Policy under the Busia government. An important feature of the second rural development programme was the co-ordination of the activities of all departments and organizations involved in youth and rural development — the integrated approach to rural development. Some of the projects tackled were schools, shops, health and community centres, rural/cottage industries and rural water supply.

The rationale underlying the 1969 Youth and Rural Development Policy, in short, was to develop the rural areas and make the lot of the inhabitants better. It was, however, not successfully implemented by the Progress Party Government of Dr. Busia. As Dorvlo (1980:10) explained;

> An integrated rural development programme is to all intents and purposes an egalitarian programme...but those who had formulated it did not believe in egalitarianism and therefore, could not adopt the measures necessary for the successful implementation aimed at promoting it.

It must, however, be noted that the time available for the implementation of the policy was short-lived. The Busia government was overthrown barely within two years of its existence.

The success or failure of rural development programmes depends on the commitment of the government in power and the level of educational awareness and involvement of the local people. Rural or community development is an indispensable factor in globalization and must be tackled. Communities need a certain level of education to accept and support the development programmes. It was with this hindsight that the decentralization policy was more effectively implemented in Ghana towards the end of the 1980s.

The Decentralization System in Ghana

In Ghana, the tempo of decentralization became faster towards the end of the 1980s to prepare people to withstand the pressure of global demands on development.

A more bold and pragmatic approach to community development in Ghana was adopted in 1988 to strengthen the local government system. The Provisional National Defence Council (PNDC) government promulgated the Local Government Law, PNDC Law 207, which created 110 District Assemblies. These have become the highest political and administrative authorities at the district level to implement an effective decentralization policy.

Under the decentralization policy, the administration of Ghana is organized on a five-tier system. At the top level are the central government and the regional co-ordinating councils. At the third level of government are the metropolitan, municipal or the district assemblies. At the fourth level are the town, zonal or area councils. Under L.I. 1989, the Unit Committee is the basic level in the local government system. A Unit is made up of communities living in a geographical area with a population of 500 people in a rural area and 1,500 in an urban area. The system works from below through to the top. There is a close link between every two levels. The basic principles underlying the system are participation and consultation at each level horizontally and among them vertically (NCCE 1998). The reasons for the implementation of the decentralization policy are shown below.

Aims of the Decentralization Policy
Development of New Power and Personality Structures
One of the basic aims of the decentralization programme is to strengthen the human resource of the districts. All along, power had been centralized at the national capital. Both political and economic power is now decentralized under the new system. A core of new leadership emerges. Assemblymen and the new administrators are trained to acquire new

skills to account for their stewardship. The decentralization policy also offers opportunity to community members to become assemblymen, councilors and unit committee members. It provides opportunities for the training of community leaders to initiate and support the development process.

District assemblies relieve the central government of the pressure of dealing with small problems of local concern. The central government thus has the opportunity to concentrate on wider national and global issues. Moreover, communities are empowered to be sensitive to their own needs. Communities are then able to become aware of their need to improve upon their own skills and environment. They become aware that they need roads, potable water and income generation activities to improve upon their standard of living.

Communities are empowered to mobilize material resources to improve conditions in their environment. They mobilize different types of taxes to develop communities. These are the origins of special levies, tolls at road barriers, property rates, licenses on drinking bars and stores and fund raising activities especially, at festivals.

Festivals have thus become tourist attractions with a variety of activities to attract and satisfy different categories of people. During festivals, local resources and small-scale industries are identified and later developed. Non-governmental organizations are also contacted to support development programmes. Communities begin to organize their tourism potentials to generate funds towards development. Cape Coast, which is termed the "Heart of Tourism" in Ghana, has developed tourist attractions such as the Kakum National Park and Game Reserve, Cape Coast Castle, Centre for National Culture and the many hotels like the Coconut Beach Hotel and the Cape Coast Hotel.

The Common Fund is made available by the central government to districts to help communities to supplement local development efforts. Specific grants from the national government are also given to communities to support local efforts for specific projects not covered by the Common Fund or to complete projects started by communities. All Members of Parliament are also given a share of the Common Fund to support their constituencies' projects of their choice.

Another important reason for the introduction and implementation of the new local government system is to enhance the provision of utility services. These include the building of health centres, recreational facilities, schools, markets, water and sanitation in all districts. The idea is to promote equitable development of all parts of the country. The development gap between the urban and rural areas is expected to be bridged by this arrangement. All sections of the community must, in one way or the other, develop and enjoy the good services of the world and participate in the global development process.

Security measures have been put in place in all districts to protect the development process. Family and community tribunals, community watchdog committees and police posts have been set up to maintain law and order to ensure peace and development.

The decentralization system of government calls for a new form of education to train personnel to man the system. It is also to prepare people to fit into the national and global political, social and economic systems. People must be trained to become leaders, producers and exporters, organizers and responsible citizens. The National Board for Small-Scale Industries (NBSSI), a non-formal education institution, was, for example, established in 1985 (Act 434) to provide the necessary education to enhance the growth of micro and small-scale business in the communities. The policy document on NBSSI deals with the following issues:

1. It makes provision for interest rates, tax systems and infrastructure development for the local industries.

2. The Technology Development section sets up funds to develop indigenous technologies.

3. The Product and Market Development provides for the dissemination of information on the domestic market and potential investment opportunities both internally and externally.

4. Inter-Industry Linkages and Networking helps to improve the

capacity of micro-and small-scale enterprises (MSEs) for effective networking and collaboration. It also identifies special target groups and improves the capacity of District Assemblies and other local authorities to link producers of industrial raw materials to MSEs.

5   The Women Entrepreneurship Development section promotes the establishment of fora for networking among women MSE operators and planning for gender-based projects for women.

6   Micro and Small Enterprise Financing strengthens the structure and operational capabilities of MSEs through training, mobilization of savings and improving credit delivery to MSEs to the Export Development and Investment Fund. It also improves MSE perception of banks and encourages banks to formulate MSE financing policy and create MSE desks.

7   Non-Financial Support Programme promotes enterprise culture, counselling and guidance for self-employment. It incorporates entrepreneur training at all levels and provides training in programme designing and implementation management skills and effective interaction between science and technology institutions, non-governmental organizations (NGOs) and MSEs (NBSSI, 94).

To accelerate the growth of MSEs, Business Advisory Centres (BACs) were set up in the regional capitals of Ghana to carry out outreach programmes of the Board. The BACs have thus become catalysts in the business promotion programmes in the District Assemblies. As a result, indigenous and small-scale business operations have been initiated and developed throughout the country. Small-scale business operators generally, through training, understand their working environment, know how to plan, design and implement projects, manage and control their finances, formulate and adopt effective market strategies and form viable co-operatives. These are some of the basic requirements for running small-scale business. The range of manufactured goods have expanded covering agriculture, industry and the services sector.

Indigenous technologies in oil extraction, pomade and soap making, weaving, pottery and basketry are revived and improved. Agriculture, in all its forms, is modernized. Batik, tie and dye, sewing and hair dressing businesses are booming because of the training provided by NBSSI to small-scale industrialists.

CONCLUSION

The technical capacities and the human resources of communities, district assemblies and unit committees must, however, be strengthened and developed on continuous bases to enhance their maximum performance. Non-formal education must equip assembly and unit committee members with the techniques for community mobilization and improvement. These members need assessment skills, tendering and supervision of contracts and adequate record keeping skills. Briefly put, members of the new structures have to be regularly enlightened on some basic principles of the system so that they can work effectively.

Two crucial issues of development with factors accounting for them have been discussed. There is a migration trend towards the urban centres because of the attractions of the cities. Migration is also due to the unavailability of jobs in the rural areas. Chieftaincy, a factor in community development is weak. The vain promises of some politicians and the various taxes imposed on people have made the people despondent to develop their own area. The world economic crisis falls heavily on governments to take strategies to revive rural development programmes. New strategies have been adopted to solve these problems. These include rural development strategies with emphasis on decentralization.

Rural people may derive some benefits from chieftaincy and other institutions. They may also benefit from government development policies and strategies. But these benefits fail to solve rural development problems. The gap between the urban and rural areas widens and remains central to rural development. The crucial issue is that the majority of people live in rural areas. They are dehumanized by illiteracy and ignorance. They cannot participate in the development process without any educational interventions from outside.

Blueprint approach to development whereby development plans are drawn at the top and implemented below should be reviewed. The dignity and expertise of the people need to be recognised and their views incorporated into the management planning system. It must also be noted that rural people negotiate from their experience, occupation and resource base. The majority are already engaged in one occupation or the other. They must, therefore, be encouraged to identify their needs and share in the design, implementation and evaluation of participatory action. Such action, according to them, is self-generated, based on their access to productive resources and services, their labour and the continued security of that access. Briefly put, they must be involved in the rural development negotiation process through participatory rural appraisal. Local initiatives and actions regenerated as a result, become important elements in rural development. Participatory management and training schemes on local initiatives need to be reorganised to improve indigenous technical know-how. Small gains in the rural industry must be consolidated and expanded through non-formal education.

In conclusion, it can said that for development to succeed, certain sectors of the economy need to be seriously examined and reorganized. The critical sector is agriculture. Agriculture must be modernized through effective planning of non-formal education strategies. Improvement in agriculture production is not however, enough in the search for positive change for the majority of rural people. Innovative practices in mobilizing rural communities to participate in reviving the fortunes of local trades must be initiated. This initiative will provide new and improved working opportunities for the under-employed manpower and under-utilized rural labour.

Chapter 4

NON-FORMAL EDUCATION AND ITS LINKAGE WITH DEVELOPMENT

Non-formal Education in Traditional African Societies

The practice of non-formal education has long been in existence, in African societies. This form of education is practised in different forms. Families play very important roles using non-formal education to prepare members for life and work. The traditions of society are transmitted, through the process of socialization, by the family to succeeding generations. The family has thus become a transmission belt which keeps alive society's culture.

The youth learn skills at home, in the marketplace and on the farm from their parents and neighbours. Special non-formal education structures are also established by traditional societies to train the youth to fit into the society. Almost every Ghanaian community is noted for a specific popular festival or cultural activity aimed at transmitting her values in all aspects of life to her citizens. Some of these festivals include the Homowo of the Ga, Aboakyir of the Efutu, Hogbetsotso of the Anlo, Damba of the Dagbon, Asafotu among the Adas and Apoo among the Wenchi and Techiman people. There is also the Kundum of the Nzema and the Ahanta. Yam festivals are celebrated among yam farming communities all over the country.

These festivals are non-formal education institutions meant to prepare individuals to play meaningful roles in society. All the festivals in one way or the other, teach the history of communities, environmental cleanliness, respect for elders, parents, family members and traditional authority. They lay emphasis on marriage and parental, family and community responsibilities. During festivals, people put on their special clothes bought for the occasion. Drumming and dancing which are necessary aspects of all festivals teach morals, bodily exercise and culture of the people. Musketry trains people in the art of bravery and equips celebrants with skills for the defence of the community. Before the D-day, compounds, water fetching points, public places of convenience and the environment are generally cleaned. Family problems, land and chieftaincy disputes are resolved. People work hard to procure food and drinks. Women prepare delicious meals. Feasting together enhances the essence of communal living and traditional hospitality.

Some of the festivals last for at least a week and are planned in such a way that provision is made to teach community values like honesty, discipline, the love for hard work, good neighbourliness and decency. Marriages are arranged by families for their members. Individuals begin to plan development activities like building or renovating the family house to accommodate visitors and friends. An influential citizen or government official is invited to dilate on national or international issues like the general elections or the world economic crisis. People must be abreast with local and international events. Festivals have become tourist potentials for communities to generate funds for community improvement activities as many tourists participate in these festivals.

Chiefs, the custodians of culture and the embodiment of those citizens dead, alive or yet to be born, dress in traditional attire to signify the culture and unity of their people. The sitting arrangement of chiefs and elders demonstrates power structure. The position of chiefs as community models of peace and unity, the embodiment of people and symbol of culture and development is established and recognized. Drum language and chief's appellations remind people about the dignity of the chief. Singing of heroic exploits of ancestors and of state heroes inspires all present to achieve greater laurels for the state. Festivals provide occasions for homecoming, tradition and culture promotion, development planning, social contacts and dispute settlement. Communities, during festivals, are brought together to develop a sense of unity and thus communities become peaceful, strong and powerful basic units for development. Together, they plan and execute community development projects like construction of school buildings following the launching of an appeal for funds.

Societies such as the Agbadjigbeto in Benin, the Poro and Sande for boys and girls in Sierra Leone respectively, the Nupe in Nigeria and the Asafo companies for the youth in Ghana, all use non-formal education to socialize members. Non-formal education programmes of these associations equip members with occupational skills relevant to the maintenance of their societies. They also learn techniques to defend their communities. The initiates and members of these groups are kept in seclusion where they learn the occupations, history, culture and laws of their societies. There are usually elders who handle them in the various subjects. The Krobo and Ewe in Ghana, use initiation ceremonies like *Dipo* and *Gbortowɔwɔ* respectively to prepare girls to play useful roles in society. The initiates learn to work, take care of their husbands, relatives and children while in seclusion prior to the initiation ceremony.

Members of some of these groups, as it is among the Poro of Sierra Leone, are sent into the bush at the dead of the night for some rituals and exercises. They, at times, take part in drills and difficult tasks. They learn to work together most of the time. The essence of these programmes is to make initiates courageous, strong and patriotic. They are to develop a sense of initiative and solidarity, all in the interest of personal and community development. Graduates of these "schools" leave to take up occupations like farming, hunting and the crafts in the community. The success of these non-formal education programmes depends on the wisdom with which they are planned and implemented.

Apprenticeship constitutes the most universal form of non-formal education in traditional African societies. Apprenticeship is the traditional system of vocational training. It is a skill acquisition scheme and the oldest form of teaching and learning a trade. An important feature of the system is that it is flexible and easily adapts to social change. That is one reason why it has survived centuries of economic and social change.

It is an effective way of ensuring that there is always a core of trained artisans and other categories of workers in the community. An advantage of the apprenticeship system is that it promotes community trades and relies mainly on local materials in vocational training and work. It, therefore, reflects the traditional economic and social concerns and aspirations of a people. It focuses training on vocations like farming, carpentry, black and gold-smithing, weaving and masonry. Other vocations include painting, fishing, hunting, pottery and carving. It thus has a great potential for employment creation and diversification of local employment opportunities. Apprentices in these jobs are provided with long-term jobs. They thus contribute towards the rural development process.

Training takes an informal nature. It is based on the principle of learning by observing and doing. Apprentices observe the techniques used by the more experienced workers. They ask questions where they are in doubt and copy their seniors as they work.

According to Smutylo (1973), apprenticeship is a disciplined institution although training takes an informal nature. Every workshop has its code of conduct to enhance discipline and hard work. The relationship in the workplace is hierarchically structured. The master-craftsman is the chief executive of the centre. He is given all the respect an elderly in society deserves. The senior apprentices work directly under him and they are the supervisors. Seniority among the apprentices is based on length of service, skill acquisition, knowledge and practice in the trade. Responsibilities are shared according to seniority. Juniors run errands, sweep the workshop, do menial jobs and hold items for the seniors to work on. Much room is provided for social mobility in the system. Junior and new apprentices in the workplace learn to submit to authority. As they become seniors they learn to wield power and take responsibilities that go with it.

Social values and responsibilities are also taught during training. In the course of the apprenticeship, trainees undertake communal labour and attend community meetings. Communal labour may involve the construction of schools and clearing of paths to public places. Apprentices are sent on errands to purchase items and know where to get equipment for the workshop. They learn to deal with customers by observing their masters perform the process. They take part in community activities such as festivals.

As apprentices become more experienced they test their competencies in jobs in the community. They learn to save money from jobs they do on their own or from the tips they receive from their masters or customers. Apprentices learn not only trade but also about community living and are prepared to serve the community in communal work, civic education and leadership positions.

When the time of training is over and the master tradesman is satisfied that the apprentices are competent, a graduation day is fixed. Elders and other tradesmen perform the graduation ceremony after which they offer pieces of advice to the trainees who are then initiated to become responsible citizens and workers in the community. Some graduands are rewarded with tools by their masters for commitment to work or obedience. Others are supported in kind or in cash by relations and friends to start their business. The rest who cannot get any support to establish their businesses undertake some post-apprenticeship employment with their master-craftsmen to get them organized so that they will later set up their own workshops.

Non-formal education has been mentioned in various ways as a tool for updating the skills of people and also socializing them to become useful citizens. But one would ask, what is meant by non-formal education, a term which is repeatedly used in this book?

THE CONCEPT OF NON-FORMAL EDUCATION

Although non-formal education has long been practised in various forms, the entry of the concept has been new and it is subject to various definitions. Writing in 1962, Batten extensively used informal education to refer to what may be aptly described as non-formal education.

The term non-formal education was developed and popularized by Coombs when he extensively used it in his books, *"The World Education Crisis: A System's Analysis"* (1968), and *"Attacking Rural Poverty: How Non-formal Education Can Help"* (1974). He described non-formal education as all those activities differently called "adult education", "on-the-job training" and "accelerated training". He believed it was a complement to the formal system and included all organized educational activities carried on outside the formal school system for specific target groups to solve immediate problems.

Variations exist in the definitions owing to the complex nature of the content of non-formal education. Simkins (1977) briefly defines it as out of school education. It is "non-school" education.

The common elements running through the definition of non-formal education by various authors including Coombs (1968), Kinsey and Bing (1978), Bown and Tomori (ed. 1979) and Fordham (1980) are that non-formal education includes all organised educational programmes outside the formal school system. Such programmes are directed towards specific target groups especially the marginalized. These activities help to develop the skills and behaviour of all categories of people so that they can find out things for themselves and make a meaning out of their lives. As the concept gained currency, many schools of thought began to support and promote it. These are discussed presently.

Replacement Education
Proponents of the non-formal idea as replacement education include the "Deschoolers" like Illich (1972) and Reimer (1972). They are very critical of the formal school system because according to them, it tends to produce people who do not fit as change agents in the social system and are not productive either. Schools have been maintained as reproductive systems producing people just to fit into the existing social system. They are to reproduce and maintain the status quo. Schools, to them, are becoming irrelevant institutions which woefully provide improper methods of teaching, writing, reading and numeracy. They only provide opportunities for compulsory mis-education. The school system must, therefore, be reorganized and re-established to respond to local needs.

The "Deschoolers" have recommended an alternative or replacement education system which should replace the formal system. This is non-formal education which can address individual, community and wider development issues.

Supplement Education
Also, there are the educational planners who want to make use of non-formal education to help settle those who earlier on benefited from some training. As part of Ghana's Economic Recovery Programme for instance, educational planners have embarked upon labour redeployment exercises. A Redeployment Management Committee which is educationally oriented was established. This committee provided

counselling services for the re-deployed to undertake non-formal education programmes. Vocational centres including pilot training centres at Ho in the Volta Region, Yamfo Vocational Training Centre in the Brong Ahafo Region, Tamale Vocational Training Institute in Northern Region, Nandom Practical Vocational Centre in the Upper West Region and Anglican Vocational Training Centre in Zuarungu in the Upper East Region have been commissioned to give non-formal education in the trades to the re-deployees. Some of the courses offered at these centres include electronics, carpentry, welding; masonry, construction, dressmaking, cooking and weaving. Without resort to non-formal education, it will be difficult to resettle them. It is in view of the above that a school of thought believes non-formal education is supplementary education, providing additional educational opportunities to people. One of the educational planners who considers non-formal education as supplementary education is Fordham (1980).

Complementary Education
There is another school of thought which sees non-formal education as a education complementary to the formal system. Among the proponents of this school is Coombs (1968). There are some activities which are not given much attention by the school curriculum. Such activities are termed extra-curricular activity. But they are necessary components of the education system and may be embodied in the school curriculum to make the system holistic. Agriculture which is the main activity in developing countries must be embodied adequately in the school curriculum to make the system complete. Sporting, drama and cultural studies also complement the educational system and are easily provided by non-formal education. Life skills, cultural and community education must be essential components of the curricula.

Liberation/Empowerment Education
Furthermore, another school of thought considers non-formal education as liberation or empowerment education. Nyerere and Freire are the great proponents of this school. To them non-formal education is to arouse the awareness of people about their oppression, poor conditions, poverty and ignorance. Non-formal education is to create the awareness

67

to help them reflect more seriously on their conditions. This the proponents believe will help people to develop themselves and their environment and become more responsible citizens. Non-formal education will then make people difficult to drive but easy to lead now that they are liberated and can analyze political issues better. As liberated people, they can assert their rights and participate in the social, economic and political issues of their community without being manipulated.

As part of government structures in all African countries, there are agents employed to extend the services of the government to all the people, including those in remote areas. Extension workers are practitioners of non-formal education in the field. They seek to help communities develop their cultural base. They are in the various sectors of the community including health, agriculture and community development. They are always in the field organizing people to take part in workshops, sharing their technical experiences with the local people. At times they hold durbars, discussions, and conduct experiments to educate communities. These are all done outside the formal school system to liberate people from their ignorance and poverty. Their activities can be described as non-formal education. Those who belong to that school of thought believe that educators must always remember that their clientele have come from a cultural base. They have their ancestral civilization of agriculture, trade, religion and politics. They cannot compete favourably with the modern institutions in their fields. They, therefore, need to acquire new skills to understand the modern changes and improve upon whatever they are doing. Non-formal education, therefore, starts with the people's cultural base and environment for development. From that stage, they can enter the national and global stage where issues are no longer interpreted in magical terms.

NON-FORMAL EDUCATION (NFE) AS A TOOL FOR DEVELOPMENT

Non-formal education is a major tool for national development. It gives help to rural folks and urban dwellers with limited or no formal educational background, to improve upon their economic and social conditions as well as those of their communities. Through non-formal education, farmers who desperately, over the years, work on their farms for subsistence can put the same acreage of land to good use for higher yields. Tradesmen also learn to improve upon the quality of their products for higher profits.

Several examples of how non-formal education helps to change the future of less-privileged societies exist. Simkins (1977), for example, described how non-formal education was used to solve some development problems. He illustrated how within a short period of time non-formal education programmes equipped participants with skills and made them competent to work in the community and establish small-scale industries and farms on their own. Thus, he described non-formal education as a competence oriented programme. Rewards are in the form of material gains and NFE's programmes usually end up with one getting a reward. Non-formal education through the utilization of such techniques as drama, pictures, films and videotapes can challenge prevailing apathy. It can mobilize the interest of the rural folk, build their confidence and encourage participation in community development or participation in some trade. Thus, non-formal education has the tremendous potential of changing people's attitudes and improving their skills to participate in the development process.

Non-formal education has many advantages over the formal school system. It is usually organized on short-term basis to encourage those who may not have full time for formal education to participate in it. Such a short programme can benefit mothers, businessmen, top executives, doctors and many professionals to improve upon their performance. If non-formal education in statecraft is not given to new rulers, their allies and the freelance politicians, the chances are that affairs of state may be mismanaged. In brief, it should be organized at the appropriate time with the right duration at each stage, to achieve its objectives.

Specifically, NFE can be used to prepare people for jobs in the community. Local trades such as carpentry, masonry and agriculture in all forms could be given priority in the curricula. This discourages the rural-urban drift and encourages people to settle down in the community to take one job or the other and to participate in the development process. It, therefore, reduces the problem of unemployment and promotes community participation.

Non-formal education is usually planned with the people of a community whose living conditions it must suit. In more modern trends, Participatory Rural Appraisal Techniques like group and focus group discussions have been used in the attempt to identify the educational facilities needed by the people. In the end, these approaches are effective as people identify programmes as their own and consciously make efforts to sustain them, since they are involved in formulating them. The content of the programme is thus flexible. Attention is focused on setting appropriate local educational and development goals. This enhances a clear definition of educational objectives in local and national framework, and promotes community participation.

Programmes planned in NFE are tailored to suit the needs of participants. They, therefore, satisfy the needs of those who are not interested in pursuing general courses. Great use is made of local human and material resources: existing structures, resource persons and facilities in the community. Such programmes are, therefore, less expensive in terms of boarding fees, structures and sophisticated equipment and tutors. Any decent dress is accepted for classes which are held at convenient places, at times under trees or in open places. Classrooms are used in the evening when schools have closed for the day. Churches and mosques may also be used if participants find them convenient.

Since great use is made of local resources, non-formal education is appropriate in meeting local needs and community technology. It also responds to the socio-economic needs of the environment and reduces waste, delays and misuse of local resources. Non-Formal Education, therefore, uses relevant and effective teaching/learning materials and methods, promoting a good blend of didactic and practical learning to help people perform their tasks well. This method leads to balanced development of the cognitive, affective and manipulative skills of learners.

Another important aspect of Non-Formal Education is that, since it is not compulsory it is open to all without laying down difficult entry requirements. There is no age limit, sex differentiation or academic qualification. It embraces all in the community, laying emphasis on grassroots participation. In so doing, NFE attracts community members who might have been left out or dropped out of the formal school system to participate in the development process. It caters for many school drop-outs who have lost all hope for survival and personal advancement in the system.

An added advantage is that non-formal education is organized for specific groups of people at specific times to solve specific problems. If there is an outbreak of cholera in a community a programme is organized for people immediately to identify causes, symptoms, cure and prevention in the community. Doctors can benefit from an NFE programme to hurriedly prepare them to tackle the outbreak of Buruli ulcer in a community. All categories of people and workers, therefore, need it because changes in society are taking place and new instruments and equipment are being introduced. People and workers must, therefore, learn to adjust to the new conditions and handle the new equipment.

Many non-formal education programmes have been established out of great concern for the disadvantaged who might never have been catered for by the formal education system. These may be the school left-outs, minority groups, the disabled and women. Non-formal education also caters for the youth, who, without parental care desperately work under poor conditions for a pittance. The aged are also given opportunities to learn some vocation and skills necessary for their survival. It caters, in a balanced form, for all ages, sexes and social groups. Briefly put, it provides great variety and important learning opportunities to assorted sub-groups in the society.

The use of the local language largely in non-formal education is to make participation more real to the people whose educational levels are low and find a foreign language too distant from them. The use of a local language develops mutual trust and promotes positive social feeling and brotherliness, while foreign language divides people into two classes: the teachers and the learners. There is usually no effective dialogue in the adult class where foreign language is the medium of communication. With the use of the local language, however, learners actively participate in the learning process and build confidence as the discussion goes on. They are encouraged to learn faster and graduate to learn the English language.

Non-formal education relies heavily on functional literacy programmes to prepare individuals to participate more meaningfully in the political, social and economic issues affecting their lives. People learn to read, write and create their own history. It helps them take part in the decision making process and understand simple electoral procedures.

In brief, therefore, non-formal education programmes have some common characteristics. They are planned with the people and organized on short-term basis to improve conditions. They are usually locally based and make use of local human and material resources like the local facilitators and buildings. There are no strict academic qualifications for registration and participation. The time table is very flexible to enhance participation of the majority. No prescribed uniforms are required but decent dresses are recommended for participants. Participation is voluntary and the use of the mother tongue or local language is encouraged. Non-formal education programmes are organized with specific vocational groups in mind such as farmers and traders. Such programmes are geared towards addressing specific problems. At the end of the programmes, participants are awarded with certificates of participation rather than academic certificates.

THE MEDIA IN NON-FORMAL EDUCATION

The success of non-formal education is to a large extent promoted by the use of the media. The importance of non-formal education is that it reaches as many people as possible. It caters for even those in scattered and isolated areas where there are no facilities for the formal school system and where there are no experts. This is because non-formal education uses the mass media (community newspapers, pamphlets, books, magazines, radio, television, films and the postal services) to reach its clientele scattered all over the place. Both the lonely person who wants to escape from the noisy public environment and experience solitary existence and the autonomous learner who prefers to study on his own, benefit a lot from the multi-media instructional system.

The mass media, people may argue, lack the effective impact required in the exchange of ideas necessary in the teaching/learning process. The best way to achieve good results then, is to combine the media and face-to-face methods of teaching and learning. This is what non-formal programmes attempt to do. At this juncture, the role of the various components of the media in non-formal education is discussed.

Radio

Radio is one of the most effective channels of the mass media in non-formal education. The strategy used is to create radio fora. The history of radio fora started in Canada in 1941, with the establishment of Farm Radio Forum by the Canadian Broadcasting Corporation. By this programme, a series of radio programmes was broadcast to the scattered farmers of Canada. These programmes were discussed by various organized farmers' groups (Dodds 1972). The programme was very successful and many farmers improved upon their farming practices after adopting the methods broadcast and discussed.

In 1964, Ghana became the first African country to organize rural radio fora with the support of the Canadian Broadcasting Corporation. But this was without the formation of discussion groups. Now rural radio fora and fan clubs have become important features of the Ghana Broadcasting Corporation's non-formal education programme. After the broadcast and the discussions, dispensaries have been built and equipped, roads constructed, markets established, new crops or improved grains planted and new methods of farming have been introduced (Dodds *Ibid)*. Pamphlets and reports produced by the various departments and the groups concerned are also discussed. With the use of radio fora people are able to acquire new knowledge to undertake community development programmes or improve upon their occupational skills.

Films

The film is another very important extended channel in non-formal education programming. With mobile vans, educational films can be shown, interspersed with entertainment to draw the awareness of the local community to development and employment issues. People watch films on how other communities work on projects. They also learn about nutrition, health, science, agriculture, home management and family life education. The programmes can be far away in the hinterland. In rural Ghana, the whole village is attracted to watch the films. The film shows are more beneficial if the operators open a forum for the discussion of the film. The audience then asks questions and comments are passed for the benefit of all. What the audience observes in the film and discusses very easily stick in their minds for reflection and future action.

However, there are occasions when the operators just show the film and do not allow for comments from the audience. There is the danger of misinterpretation of the message of the film if the operators just show the film thus making the audience passive viewers. There is the need for the inclusion of open discussion which will lead to the successful running of non-formal education programmes through the use of the film.

Community Newspapers

Another important medium which promotes non-formal education is the community newspaper. Community newspapers are published in the local languages to make the people treasure literacy in their mother tongue. The importance of these papers is great because people enjoy reading and writing about their own activities. They also admire their own pictures in the local papers. An important feature of the local newspapers is the formation of Readers' Clubs. These Clubs are formed in the circulation zone of the paper. Communities are always kept busy writing and reading their own news to better their lot. Together they implement what they read, write and discuss. A good example of a successful newspaper is the *Kpodoga*, published by the Institute of Adult Education of the University of Ghana. The newspaper promotes the formation of Kpodoga Readers' clubs. Club members meet regularly to read, write news items and participate in community development activities as discussed in the newspaper.

Popular Theatre

Popular theatre is dramatization of local episodes mirrored back to the people. It utilizes indigenous familiar communicative systems such as town criers, drums, folk songs and local entertainment institutions like concerts, poetry, story-telling and masquerades in promoting development. It goes directly to the community in a challenging way, focusing on their problems and prospects such as shelter, food, clothing and health. It is not a play directed from above but planned by the people to entertain and educate themselves on local issues.

Popular theatre draws people's awareness to embrace non-formal education, shows what has gone wrong, what must be done, how it must be done and encourages them to take appropriate measures to improve their conditions. In any campaign for development, for example, popular theatre is a viable tool for community mobilization. It lifts up people's spirits, raises and sustains their interest. It also helps the development workers to understand more clearly why a community behaves in a particular way. This helps development workers review their developmental assumptions. Theatre is also used to analyze and evaluate non-formal education. It is cheaper than either the electronic or the print media. But theatre per se cannot be an effective tool for change. It must provide an opportunity for questions relating to the needs of the environment to be raised and discussed. It must create awareness, mobilize people and motivate them to take action; otherwise, it only becomes an interesting and exciting concert.

In various ways, the mass-media comprising films, television, newspapers, popular theatre and others can contribute to the success of non-formal education programmes in job creation and in solving other related problems. The mass media bridge the distance between the rural, isolated illiterate adults and the experts. It can reach more people easily and cheaply. In organized groups, the illiterate or those with little education can learn quickly. Though it has been observed that the processes of the print and electronic media are impersonal and ephemeral respectively, they support the work of the extension officers extensively.

In this chapter, the concept of Non-Formal Education is defined. Its practice has long been in existence. We have shown that a variety of schools of thought on NFE exists and that the focus of NFE is on participation and development. With this background information, it is worthwhile discussing in detail some related theories and practical experiments in NFE.

Chapter 5

SOME RELATED THEORIES AND PRACTICAL EXPERIMENTS IN NON-FORMAL EDUCATION IN DEVELOPING COUNTRIES

Introduction

No meaningful discussion on non-formal education and development would be complete unless potential contributions of two great practitioners of non-formal education namely, Paulo Freire and Julius Nyerere are clearly illustrated. Both educators share the same philosophy, that man is the centre of any development process. According to them human resource development should, therefore, be central in this process. This philosophy they put into practice successfully in Brazil and Tanzania respectively.

PAULO FREIRE AND THE BRAZILIAN EXPERIMENT

Paulo Freire, a Brazilian educator was born to poor parents in 1921 in Recife, in the north eastern part of Brazil. His early years were the period of world-wide economic depression. Freire suffered from real hunger during his school days. As he himself admitted, he could not cope with his studies because of hunger. He spent his early adulthood under poor conditions among artisans, farmers, fishermen and Red Indians. Many of these people were very poor. Farmers, for example, had to work on the farms of landlords for pitiful rewards. Yet, they could not complain. This was because the political, social and economic structures were organized and maintained in such a way that people believed that their suffering was destined. Because of his bitter experience of these conditions, Freire was driven by the burning desire to fight poverty, hunger, squalor, disease and ignorance wherever and

77

whenever he found them, but more particularly among the voiceless majority.

As a lecturer in the University of Brazil, Freire conducted research in collaboration with students and the local people among the poor. The use of local personnel was to de-mystify research as the domain of the academics. Research reports demonstrated the achievements of the people while at the same time they pointed out their faults to them: they worked hard to satisfy their masters, while they themselves continued to suffer without fighting for their rights.

Freire, through his studies, saw mass illiteracy as a result of structural injustice in society. This structure was built and maintained by the powerful to keep people in perpetual silence, though they lived and worked under intolerable conditions. Oppression rather than laziness was identified by him as the cause of poverty, ignorance and suffering. He contended that the culture of silence could only be contained by liberation education. This form of education has to inspire participants to take action. He, however, did not see action as a mere coping activity. To him action is a revolutionary process which leads to radical transformation of the person, the community and the society. As a result, he based his philosophy on six main principles (Freire 1985).

The Six Key Principles of Freire's Conscientization Concept

Firstly, he notes that no education is ever neutral. Education is either for domestication or liberation. While "domestication education" makes people to conform submissively to the *status quo*, "liberation education" creates the right climate for individuals to become creative, critical and responsible members of the community. The practice of any education should therefore, be a liberation one, Freire noted.

Secondly, whatever participants (especially adults) learn, have to be of immediate relevance to them. It is only when education is relevant to the needs of participants that they will be motivated to participate in the programmes designed for them. It is here that the issue of "generative themes" or issues that are of great concern to people are collected and dealt with in class. Such generative themes have to deal

with what people are happy about, worried about, sad about or un-
clear about. The themes could cover structures which limit their progress
or can enhance their development.

The third principle states that problem-posing approach should
be adopted in the education process. Freire condemns the "banking"
approach to education. By this system, the supposedly all knowing
teacher "fills" learners with issues which may not even be relevant to
their needs. But "the more completely he fills the receptacles, (the
students) the better a teacher he is; the more meekly the receptacles
permit themselves to be filled the better students they are" (Freire
1972:45). Students thus become passive objects absorbing whatever
is forced on them. Students are disciplined in the way the teacher wishes.
They have no hand in the choice and preparation of what they learn. In
brief, they are manipulated to satisfy the ends of the teacher and the
demands of the ruling class that he represents. By this approach, the
creative power of students is nipped in the bud. They cannot, therefore,
transform the world around them but fall into the logic of the existing
social, economic and political system to conform to it. In other words,
they have become domesticated and are submerged into the "culture of
silence". This is a common trend in politics when those in power use
propaganda to maintain themselves in power.

In the problem-posing approach to education that Freire advocates
and practises, the participants are recognized as intelligent people. Right
from beginning of the programme, people are taken into partnership
with the facilitator in the choice and preparation of what to learn. The
facilitator then creates the right climate for participants, and raises
questions, which help them to identify their own problems, find the root
causes of these problems and find solutions to them. The whole process
is a participatory learning technique.

This problem-posing process exposes participants to the reality
of their conditions and of the world. It develops the critical consciousness
of all to liberate themselves and transform the world around them.
Participants are thus seen actively involved in describing, analyzing,
taking decisions and action to change their situations and conditions.

Fourthly, Paulo Freire advocates that dialogue should be the
medium of education. As it is practicably impossible for one person to

build a just society, as many people as possible have to be involved in the education and development process. The talents and resources of all have to be tapped and harnessed since no one has the answers to all questions. And so also is no one completely stupid or ignorant. All have contributions to make to achieve success. A network of all existing institutions and individuals in the community must be built. The wisdom of the elders, the energy of the youth and the motherliness of women must all be brought together to promote active participation and involvement of all, goading them on to common action for development. The emphasis is on collaboration. Other stakeholders in the field have to be involved in the development process.

Fifthly, reflection and action should be a necessary component of the Participatory Rural Approach to the development process. From the initial stage of baseline studies, through the implementation and evaluation stages, participants have to analyze their achievements. Where possible, new direction may be forged to satisfy new demands and action taken to address emerging problems. In other words, at every stage of development programmes, people need time to critically analyze their successes and failures so as to see their way through more clearly. Without effective reflection, people may not appreciate the course of action chartered. Freire puts it more convincingly:

> At all stages of their creation, the oppressed must see themselves as people engaged in the vocation of becoming more fully human. Reflection leads to action but that action will only be a genuine praxis if there is critical reflection on its consequences (Freire 73:41).

Finally, all educational and development programmes have to lead to the radical transformation of life of the individuals, the community and society; in this connection, educational programmes implemented by both the facilitators and beneficiaries lead to a change in the circumstances of the beneficiaries. What Freire emphasizes is that education must improve the skills, knowledge and attitude of the individual and community members at large. A positive change in individuals and the environment is necessary at the end of the learning or development process. Freire practicalized his principles and liberated

80

the people from their culture of silence. Some of the generative themes he used were **government, food, work, plough, wealth, hoe. Afro-Brazilian dancing** and **wells**. He organized literacy classes according to the needs and vocations of the people. These cultural circles, as he called the classes, discussed the themes. The themes were decoded to show how they affected the lives of people. In the decoding, there were three main issues participants must know:

1.   that they are oppressed;
2.   that they can do something to liberate themselves;
3.   that they must take action to transform the conditions under which they live or work.

But the realization of these issues is not the end of the learning process. Participants are expected to take action to remedy the situation thus discussed. To Freire, the importance of education is its linkage with action and development. Discussion on hunger was followed by the production of food. Other discussions led to the digging of wells, learning Brazilian songs and dances, buying of new hoes, collaborating more effectively on the co-operative farm, challenging the arrogant authority of the landlord and questioning low wages and high rents. The unjust social structure was challenged. Reading and writing followed these discussions and actions.

Levels of Consciousness

Freire notes three major levels of consciousness through which the illiterate has to be taken so that he will be able to develop from the ignorant to the responsibility state. This must be achieved through constant and relevant education. The states are the following:

Naive-intransitive consciousness stage
At this level, man is only existing in the world. Man is a slave to norms, myths, values and taboos of society. Man in this state cannot understand problems around him. Changes around him mean nothing to him.

81

He is even afraid of change and his own freedom. He is so much attached to the natural world that he will not dare transform it. He may resist any forces which may bring change. He even lacks the intelligence to take part in activities that will result in changes in the community. He gives magical explanation to causes and effects of events. He cannot differentiate between education and propaganda. Petty gifts from those in authority mean so much to him. Man is made to believe that whatever happens to him is destined by nature. Persons in authority including landlords are mysterious and impersonal and cannot be challenged; and so situations are mystefied; traditional rituals and cultural celebrations mean so much to him. His interest centres on biological needs, his creative power is impaired, he moves along with others and is satisfied with this movement. He learns to adapt and adjust meekly to circumstances. The elite who are happy about this state of affairs interpret democracy to mean popular silence.

Semi-transitive consciousness state
As man takes part in liberation education and interacts with the world and others, he develops from the naïve-intransitive consciousness state to that of semi transitive consciousness state. Signs of limited change in technology, building, social patterns and relationships appeal to him. He takes local actions to meet immediate demands. The individual gradually begins to discover himself. The use of dialogue gradually opens his consciousness and expands his horizon. But he is not developed fully to take initiatives to fully liberate himself.

The critical consciousness stage
Freire notes that if the education process is continuous and consistent, man emerges from semi transitivity to the critical transitive consciousness state. At this critical point, man rejects his passive position and assumes responsibility roles; he no longer gives magical explanation to causes and effects of events. He understands the reality of his life. He becomes aware of his true social position and knows that freedom is not achieved all at once. It involves continuous struggle for liberation and he questions the poor position he has endured for long. He takes

bold action to liberate himself. Thus he actively takes part in the social economic and political issues of his community. He ensures that justice prevails (Hope and Timmel 1984).

Freire's Educational Methodology

Freire has sympathizes with the poor state of man and notes that for him to become critically conscious some strategies have to be adopted in the education process. In view of this, Freire coins and popularizes the concept of conscientization as the key concept in the educational process. Freire believes that the understanding of people, their way of life and their relationships should be the starting point of the education process. The world of work, ideas, myths, art, science, culture, local and national history all have to be studied and become the bases for the development of educational materials. The stages are briefly noted as listed below:

1. Undertaking of baseline studies/PRA in collaboration with potential learners and facilitators;

2. Development of Curriculum from data collected among communities. This has to be done from a negotiation process between the facilitator and the learners;

3. Development of education materials. (Based on generative themes collected in the field).
    (a) Primers,
    (b) Charts,
    (c) Games,
    (d) Role plays;

4. Establishment of Culture Circles to reflect social and occupational interest of participants;

5. Opening of classes at appropriate centres convenient to the different interest groups;

6. Recommended techniques in class to focus on *generative themes* arriving at the keyword:
   (a) Discussion and Dialogue (Problem-posing technique)
   (b) Use of local language.
   (c) Listening — a necessary component in the teaching process. Listening is an art and a skill and has to be developed by the facilitator;

7. Reflection and Action (Praxis): Situation-specific Development Activities (DAs) — Income-generation Activities, (IGAs);.

8. Traditional Literacy (writing, reading and numeracy) linking IGAs and DAs.

9. Follow-up: Follow-ups to avoid the tendency of people relapsing into illiteracy, with much emphasis on socio-economic development of beneficiaries (Freire 1973).

Freire, both a philosopher and educator put his philosophical concept of conscientization into practice. He organized culture circles and together with participants, they collected generative themes relating to the occupational and social interest of each group. Through debates and use of discussion of charts, role-plays and reflection, relating to the their situations, participants became aware of their basic needs. They learnt to read, write and calculate figures related to their work and life. They went further to use the literacy skills acquired to improve upon their occupation and social life. Some of the income-generation activities undertaken included farming and the handicrafts. Social activities included digging of wells, fighting for their rights and learning Brazilian culture.

Freire's programme covered a period of 40 hours after which the illiterates were conscientized. Through the mastery of syllables, participants learnt to build words. They were able to learn to write and read through the process of discovery. Discussants were no longer in the shadow of others nor were they just part of the masses but one of the people, as some of the learners themselves declared. Participants discovered their dignity and importance in society. Freire has a clearer picture of the situation and declared: "it is remarkable to see with what enthusiasm these illiterates engage in debate and with what curiosity they respond to questions implicit in the codification" (Freire 1973: 47). In the words of Odilon Rebeire Coutinho, "these detemporalized men begin to integrate themselves in time". (Freire 1973: 47) Many participants during these debates affirmed happily and self-confidently: "I am going to work with my head high. I work, and working I transform the world" (Freire 1973: 48). People realized that they were a part of the world and that their contributions helped to develop it. Freire's revolutionary educational methods lay much emphasis on reflection, action and transformation as the results of the educational process.

All over the world now, Freire's writings and techniques are well known. His techniques have been modified and applied in many countries. Popular terminologies such as **conscientization, culture of silence, dialogue, banking, empowerment** and **liberation** are associated with him. His ideas greatly influenced the thinking and work of Julius Nyerere of Tanzania.

JULIUS NYERERE AND THE TANZANIAN EXPERIMENT

Julius Nyerere also put into practice his philosophy of self-reliance backed by non-formal education, after the Arusha Declaration of 1967. Nyerere emphasized the role of man as the centre of development. The basis of it all was the Ujamaa Vijij Jini (familyhood), the villagization programmes which resettled the people in new environments to live together, learn together and work together. Non-formal education helped people to realize these objectives so that they could work on common projects like roads, schools, community centres, common shops, farms and property. Functional literacy programmes were organized and subjects included Political Education, Agriculture, Health, Home Economics and a common language, Kiswahili. In 1973, there were 2,586,702 registered participants in the classes with 1,370,000 participants for agriculture. Farmers learnt to improve upon fishing techniques, cattle rearing, rice, cotton and banana cultivation. On the whole, food production improved tremendously as a result of these programmes (Hinzen and Hundsdorfer 1979).

Nyerere (1976) used various strategies to give credence and build the viability of non-formal education. One of the most effective strategies was the integration of non-formal education programmes into the formal school system. By the Education Act of 1969, the Ministry of Education was renamed Ministry of National Education to co-ordinate all educational matters on a national level. The sharp distinction between formal and non-formal education, where both hitherto, were under different ministries, was removed. School facilities were used by non-formal education participants. The headteacher of each school was the head of the literacy class in the community. Teachers in the school were the facilitators at literacy classes. Budget allocation was made by the government to supplement the school budget for the acquisition of some equipment for adult learners. In view of these arrangements, schools were no longer considered elitist institutions.

Adult teaching methods were introduced into teacher training colleges and teacher trainees did their teaching practice in non-formal education centres. Diploma and degree courses were available in the Institute of Adult Education, University of Dar-es-Salaam to prepare professionals to work in adult education and non-formal education institutions. This arrangement was to give credence and respectability to the non-formal system as it gave to the formal system (Nyerere 1976).

A work-oriented-adult literacy programme was implemented. It was linked to vocational training, community and personal hygiene, nutrition, child-care and home economics. Primers catered for these subjects. In addition to the primers, rural newspapers, teachers' guides, rural libraries and newsletters were provided to support the programme. Radio groups were also established.

Hinzen and Hundsdorfer (1979) intimated that there were 958 community radio study groups in Tanzania. They estimated that a total of 1.5 to 2 million learners were registered members of the groups nation-wide. Two very successful radio programmes to millions of adults were Mtu ni afya (Man is Health) and Chakula ni Uhai (Food is

Life). It was noted that many Radio study groups undertook thousands of projects. Some groups started growing vegetables like lettuce, cabbage and tomatoes. There were others who undertook fishing and poultry-keeping. The rest opened day-care centres for children and canteens for workers. Educational elements were necessary components of these projects.

Apart from the projects undertaken, the groups tackled the problems associated with food production and food consumption. Issues of poor nutrition, poor health, poor work and low productivity were addressed. The establishment of folk development colleges institutionalized the gains of non-formal education in Tanzania.

Folk Development Colleges

Another bold attempt made by Nyerere in the Tanzania non-formal education experiment to arrest the high rate of unemployment and accelerate the tempo of participation in rural development was the establishment of Folk Development Colleges. These colleges in Tanzania were versions of the Nordic Folk High Schools but were designed to suit Tanzania's needs. They were to provide practical lessons as a follow-up to the literacy programme which by 1975 enrolled about 5.2 million participants. Courses were organized in agriculture, pottery, sewing, weaving, shop-keeping, carpentry and almost all available trades and occupations in the various local areas. One college was sited in each of the 85 districts. Many of the schools were successfully maintained.

It is worthwhile to give a brief illustration of one of the colleges. At Bigma, "FDC had cultivated a 26 acre farm, a two acre vegetable garden, cattle and pig keeping, a shop, a cookery project, a sewing project for making shirts, trousers, blouses and shirts" (Fordham 1980 : 85). Profits realized from the projects amounted to She 28,000.

The intake of students at various colleges ranged from 40 to 160, depending on availability of accommodation. The importance of these non-formal education projects was shown by their results. The majority of graduates settled in the rural areas and established their own trades and vocations. They contributed to the development of their communities.

Not surprisingly, however, some of the graduates of these colleges who were supposed to establish businesses on their own moved to the urban areas looking for white-collar jobs. They assumed that the certificates received were meant to help them to look for jobs.

Some of the non-formal education programmes in Tanzania were not as successful as originally planned. However, the enthusiasm with which the ideas were received and the philosophy underlying them can be justified.

Tanzania in the colonial days were two countries — Tanganyika and Zanzibar. The people of Tanzania have, over the centuries, suffered terribly from their enemies, including the Portuguese invaders and colonizers. Then came the Arabs and the Zulus. There were a series of slave wars and also the slave trade in the 19th century. The 1880s were noted for the German colonization which resulted in one of the severest rebellions in colonial history, the Maji maji revolts which were quelled with unprecedented severity by the Germans. When the British took over the administration of Tanzania after the First World War, they exploited rather than reconstructed the country in the Mandate Period (1919–1946).

Thus, at the end of World War I, the population of Tanzania was really under-developed in several respects. Many of the people who lived in scattered settlements had accepted apathy and political indifference as their way of life – a lesson their long history of surrender had taught them (Hinzen and Hundsdorfer 1979:3).

It is against this background that non-formal education and its successful linkage with development may be justified in Tanzania. The people have been brought together; they conquered fear and developed a sense of confidence and self-reliance; they have been equipped with skills to develop themselves and the environment. Their lives have become more meaningful to them. They learnt some trade, improved upon their lives and participated in the reconstruction of their country. They began to participate in global issues and the founder of the nation was vocal on international platforms. The one party state introduced by Nyerere disrupted some of the gains of non-formal education since it was imposed. In the next chapter, we will look at the non-formal education programmes in Ghana.

Chapter 6

GHANA'S NATIONAL NON-FORMAL EDUCATION PROGRAMME

Introduction

Adult literacy, a vital component of non-formal education, was initially introduced into the then Cold Coast (now Ghana) in 1451 by the Portuguese Catholics. The activities of the slave raiders disrupted the programme which collapsed without any impact on the people. It was re-introducted in the 18th century by Jacobus Kapitein (1717–1747) of the Dutch Reformed Church. The fortunes of literacy and Christian religion were in the doldrums until the 19th century when they were revived by a host of missionary societies. Among the early arrivals were the Basel Missionary Society (Presbyterians) (1828), and the Wesleyan Missionary Society (1835). In 1847, the Bremen Missionary Society from Germany settled in the Volta Region and reduced the Ewe language to reading and writing. This society translated the Bible into Ewe and started literacy programmes among converts. Moral and Christian principles were the main issues taught.

EXPERIMENTAL LITERACY PROGRAMME

The British Colonial Government did not participate in the literacy programme until, after the Second World War in 1948. By the Education Ordinance of 1948, the government officially incorporated literacy into the national education system. Dr Frank Laubach, an American who had a track record in developing and mounting a literacy package (the Laubach Technique) in the Philippines was invited by the government to start the national literacy programme on a pilot basis in four regions namely Volta (1948–1949) Central, Western and Ashanti (1949–1951).

First National Literacy Programme,1951–1968

In 1951, the gains of the pilot programme influenced the Legislative Assembly to approve a plan for Mass Literacy and Mass Education under the Department of Social Welfare and Community Development. The Mass Education Officers were trained in the Laubach teaching method in the first quarter of 1952. The national literacy programme, therefore, officially started after the training of the instructors in 1952. The Mass Education Officers became the supervisors of the literacy classes (Sautoy 1960).

Literacy committees mobilzed learners and recruited voluntary instructors. Classes and community development activities were organised throughout the length and breadth of the country. Unfortunatey, however, literacy programmes declined shortly after the fall of the Convention People's Party (CPP) government in 1966. The collapse of the programme was due to several reasons. The programme was associated with the CPP government because some classes discussed Nkrumaism. Many of the classes were facilitated by CPP activists. Facilitators were no longer prepared to offer voluntary services. They preferred salary payment to the award of certificates and badges for services rendered. Other reasons for the decline of the mass literacy campaign included the following:

1. Low academic level of some of the facilitators who did not know the grammar of the languages they were teaching;

2. Appropriate reading materials for literacy work were lacking;

3. Content of primers was not related to the immediate concerns and needs of participants. Christian religious values were taught in traditional religious environments;

4. The Laubach method which was used failed to actively involve learners in discussions. The facilitators used the banking method of teaching;

5. Composition of classes by putting men, women and youth together discouraged full participation by the various groups. By tradition, women and the youth do not raise issues in the presence of men;

6   Lack of follow -up reading materials made people relapse into illiteracy and discouraged class attendance;

7   There was a shortage of reading materials for beginners.

The period from 1966 to 1986 marked the era of free market approach to literacy. Churches and voluntary organizations competed in the field to establish literacy classes. The majority of these classes adopted a generalistic approach to literacy work. Learners were exposed to traditional/basic literacy but not to functional literacy programmes (Blunch and Porter 2003).

The Second National Literacy Programme, 1987–2002

The Provisional National Defence Council (PNDC) government realized the need for non-formal education towards human resource development in the country. It, therefore, made provision for it in its 1986 Education Reform Programme. As a result, the Non-Formal Education Division of the Ministry of Education was created in 1987 under PNDC Law 48. This Division of the Ministry was to co-ordinate all non-formal education related activities in the country. The implementation of the programme started with two pilot areas in Winneba/Apam in the Central Region and Tono/Vea in the Upper East Region between November 1989 and March 1991.

Objectives of the Non-Formal Education Division

Main Objective
The main objective of the Non-Formal Education Division was to provide opportunities for people, especially, the poor and women in communities to benefit from functional literacy programmes to improve upon their

livelihood and participate in community development activities (NFED 1999a: 2).

Specific Objectives were

1   To enable participants to better meet their personal and social needs through enhancing their abilities to deal competently with problems of everyday life in a literate environment;

2   To enable learners to improve upon their occupational skills through functional literacy;

3   To equip learners with knowledge, attitude and skills (KAS) that will enable them raise the quality of life in their communities;

4   To broaden the reading interest of learners and establish an attitude of reading for pleasure through the provision of follow-up literacy materials (NFED *Ibid* : 3).

The programme was to build a literate society where people would be aware of what was happening not only in their environment but also in the world at large. They were expected to stop depending on donor support and learn to be independent through the use of occupational and life skills acquired in class.

In view of the importance of functional literacy to the nation's development, resources which were committed to the National Functional Literacy Programme were in consonance with the developmental objectives of the country. It had a national character with the aim of achieving national results. It is to build a literate society where people would acquire skills to participate in the development process and be linked to the world at large.

The first phase of the programme lasted officially for six years (1992–1997). It had a target population of 5.6 million adult illiterates and 2.8 million youth as at 1987 when it was started. At the end of the first phase of the programme, the national illiteracy rate was reduced from 69 per cent in 1984 to 52 per cent in 1997. An average of 200,000 learners benefited from the literacy programme annually from 1992 to 1997. One million and two hundred people graduated from the classes at the end of the first phase. (NFED 1999b).

Operational Policies of the Functional National Literacy Programme

The following major operational policies guide the Non-Formal Education Division in the implementation of its programmes to enhance the realization of its objectives in the second phase of the programme.

1. Basic literacy management

    A class is to consist of an average of 25 learners. Each class is to be managed at the community level by a Literacy Advisory Committee. The Committee is charged with the responsibility of meeting at least once a month to discuss class problems, monitor facilitator/learner participation, encourage learner/facilitator in community development activities and provide an attractive incentive package.

2. The facilitator

    The literacy facilitator, a resident of the community, must be at least 18 years old. He must hold a minimum of Basic Education Certificate or School Certificate or their equivalents.

3. Completion of literacy cycle

    A class cycle is considered duly completed after 21 months when at least 80 per cent of the registered learners have completed the course. All learners who are able to complete the cycle irrespective of sitting for or passing the assessment test are deemed qualified to earn certificates provided their class records indicate good performance.

4. Facilitator incentive package

In the first phase of the programme, a facilitator was rewarded with either a bicycle or a sewing machine. Under the second phase, a variety of items including a bicycle, sewing machine, wax prints, cement and roofing sheets are some of the packages a facilitator can choose from.

5. Facilitator and supervisor training

All new facilitators are to benefit from two types of training. These are the 14-day initial training which is organised at the beginning of the cycle, and the 7-day refresher training within the cycle, Retained facilitators benefit from a 7-day training at the beginning of the cycle. The supervisor undergoes a 7-day training in the first two years of the programme and a second training in the fourth year.

6. Scope of supervision responsibility and frequency of supervision visits

A supervisor, an employee of the NFED, is to visit each class in his zone at least once every month. He/she is expected, among other responsibilities, to check the facilitator attendance and evaluate both the facilitator and learners' participation and performance in class.

7. Monitoring, evaluation and research

The Monitoring, Evaluation and Research Unit plans effective monitoring, evaluation and research of the NFLP activities. Data base management systems set up with the help of a computer programmer handle the production of training materials and processing of data.

8. Income-generation activities

    Focus will be placed on the training of income-generation groups in collaboration with NGOs and CBOs. Groups which solicit support from NFED are however, to operate viable bank accounts at least for one year, and obtain a minimum of 60 per cent class attendance and have a ready source of raw materials within the district or locality for their project.

9. English pilot classes

    English classes will be opened in communities subject to the availability of facilitators and neo-literates, and suitable meeting place. Since some of the lessons will be supported by Radio programme, the class must have access to FM broadcasts from NFED stations and collaborators. English literacy programmes lasting 20–30 minutes will be broadcast twice a week to supplement class face-to-face instructions. 920 classes will be opened on pilot basis throughout the country.

10. Creation of literate environment

    It is important to keep learners and neo-literates in literacy tune. For this reason, a number of programmes are to be put in place to reorganize the provision of reading materials.

    *   Easy-to-read story books to be produced by the Ghana Book Publishers;
    *   Learner – produced materials;
    *   Community newspapers; and
    *   Materials to be purchased from other literacy providers.

    All these policies are implemented and are on-going to make the programme a success.

95

Stages in the NFLP

Two basic stages exist in the programme. These are Basic Literacy and Post Literacy stages. However, these stages overlap in course of their implementation.

1. **Basic Literacy Stage**: Conditions are created for learners to develop the habit for creative thinking, the anxiety for objective analysis, the ambition for inquiry and the curiosity for innovation. At this stage, learners acquire functional knowledge, develop positive attitude to life, adopt appropriate skills to work and exhibit analytical and problem solving skills. They learn to read and write in the local language and calculate simple figures relating to their daily transactions.

2. **Post – Literacy Stage:** At this stage, the status of the neo-literates is enhanced as a result of the acquisition of some skills and knowledge. They become independent learners and access other learning materials relevant to their life and work. Some of them join English classes. Neo-literates read for leisure and pleasure. General reading and class activities are reinforced by radio programmes which highlight the various developmental, economic and social issues in the primer. Social problems in the community are also discussed in the radio programmes.

    Neo-literates take more active part in the social activities of their communities. They play effective roles in social groups such as women and youth associations. They more willingly either initiate or actively take part in development and income – generation activities.

Curriculum Design

The essence of the functional literacy programme is mainly to provide learning opportunities to participants to acquire occupational skills, get access to income-generation activities and improve their lifestyles in the modern social system. The programme is, therefore, organized to respond to the social, economic and political needs of the people. The contents of the primer focus on three areas:

— Civic education
— Environment and health
— Income-generation

Civic education

By civic education programmes, the awareness of individuals is drawn to their rights and responsibilities as citizens. Everybody is expected to participate in local and national development issues. The dignity of individuals and the rights of children are to be respected. The institution of chieftaincy is to be given the due recognition and respect to ensure stability and development of communities. Taxes and levies are to be paid so as to build the economy, while expensive funerals which deprive bereaved families of the little resources at their disposal are to be discouraged.

Environment and Health

The focus in this session is on life skills. Environmental and social problems such as poor sanitation, bush burning, drug abuse, teenage pregnancy, population growth, unsafe drinking water and mortality exist in communities. Modern medical facilities are limited while traditional medicine is indiscriminately patronized by communities. The AIDS menace is spreading fast, but communities do not take precautionary measures to avoid it. The topics dealing with health and social issues, therefore, draw people's attention to the problems that endanger their lives and suggest ways and means to help them enjoy healthy lives.

Income-Generation

The focus of the Functional Literacy Programme is to equip rural people with occupational skills so that they can be integrated into the main stream of modern economic life. For this reason, provision is made in the primer and the programme to cater for a variety of occupational needs of communities. Lessons are taught on modern methods of animal husbandry and farming. Specific chapters deal with skill acquisition in cocoa farming, dry season gardening, oil palm cultivation and bee-keeping. Women learn to smoke, preserve and market fish for more profit. Provision is also made in the primer to cater for the occupational and educational needs of those engaged in handicrafts such as pottery and basket weaving. Lessons learnt in class discussion of the topics are put into practice in the field. Some credit facilities are also given to learners who engage in economic activities.

Each of the topics in the primer is illustrated with a composite picture depicting issues raised. Discussion of the picture leads to the identification of the key word and syllabization. Meaningful words are formed and sentences are constructed from the words. Development activities are undertaken and discussed in class as will be shown later.

Administration and Implementation of the Programme

The Division has its headquarters in Accra with 10 regional offices and 110 district offices. Each district is divided into zones. Each zone is made up of at least 15 classes under a zonal supervisor. There are 1200 zones operated by NFLP nationwide. The District co-ordinator and staff and in particular, the zonal supervisors are to offer the facilitator support in facilitating learning, class management, implementation of development and income-generation activities. The Literacy Advisory Committee and the Class Management Committee are set up at all levels to provide advice and support the smooth running of the programme.

In 1989, government adopted the use of the modified Freirean participatory approach for the program. Discussions are interspersed with the use of picture cards, picture codes, games, stories, proverbs, role-plays and drama to illustrate issues in more detail. Songs are also used to reinforce lessons. These techniques arouse and sustain people's interest in participating in class activities, build their confidence and empower them to identify and solve their own problems. Friendly an cordial relationships are also developed during discussions.

Each viable class in the country constitutes a radio forum known as a Radio-Listening Group and is provided with a pre-set radio. Topics in the primers are produced jointly by NFED and Ghana Broadcasting Corporation and transmitted to learners, facilitators, supervisors and the general public. The richness of the radio programmes could be found in the variety of examples and different voices of presenters in addition to those of the facilitators. Facilitators are reminded of teaching techniques and ideas to adopt in the field. The recorded activities, comments and other views of different groups of learners are played back to all to build a network of learners. These recorded programmes inspire the feeling of belongingness and motivation to participate in the programmes as well as reinforce learning activities of participants. The audience who are not members of the classes also learn and adopt lessons from the programmes. A very popular series is on the causes, symptoms and effects of HIV/AIDS on individuals and society at large.

There is a special radio programme which deals with *Literacy News* from the regions and the districts. It provides an up-date on activities at class centres all over the country to learners, facilitators, supervisors, administrators and the general public. In addition, the classes sometimes listen to and discuss news items of other countries to know what is happening in the world at large.

A 32-page literacy comic series has been developed. These comprise illustrations and cartoons that carry various issues in the primer. They are translated and printed in the 15 operational languages. The comics are meant to break monotony of reading prose all the time. They emphasize the topics discussed in an entertaining and relaxed manner (Blunch and Porter 2003).

TRAINING

Training is a process of helping people to attain a desired standard of efficiency or behaviour. It is to help people acquire knowledge and improve performance.

Training generally benefits four categories of institutions and individuals:

1. Trainees: Training develops the attitude and skills of trainees towards performance improvement;

2. The organizations: Training promotes organizational culture, and enhances maximization of profit;

3. Consuming Public: Training ensures customer satisfaction;

4. Trainers: Training develops the competence and builds the confidence of trainers.

Training programmes, therefore, benefit trainers, trainees, the organization and the consuming public. The needs of the consuming public and the organization are studied and incorporated into the training programme. In some organizations, emphasis on training is on the promotion of the organizational culture and maximization of profit. In the Non-formal Education Division, emphasis on training is placed on its utilitarian value: Individuals are to be equipped with skills to improve upon their performance and make a meaning out of life. It is in this light that the training programmes of the NFED have been drawn. The processes adopted by NFED for the national functional literacy programme include the following;

— Identification of the training needs and concerns of the consuming public and beneficiaries;
— Formulation of training objectives of the NFLP;
— Building of training alliance with organisations with identical education and development objectives;
— Designing of training programme;
— Implementation of training programme.

The cascade approach to training using what I may conceptualise as a Snowball Model in training is adopted. A core of experienced training officers drawn from partner organizations are mobilized and

100

trained at the national, regional and district levels. At the top of the cascade is the Central Training Team (CTT). The CTT trains the Regional Training Team (RTT) while the RTT trains the District Training Team (DTT). The trend of training continues till facilitators and supervisors at the community levels are trained throughout the country.

The course content covers the Philosophy of Literacy, the History and Objectives of Ghana's Functional Literacy Programmes, the Facilitator in Literacy Delivery, the Adult Learner and Gender and Development. Other topics include Development and Income-Generation Activities. Much attention is also given to micro-teaching during all training programmes. Team members learn and practise the techniques of teaching, reading, writing and numerals.

The strategy adopted for training is a good example of the Training of Trainers (TOT) programme. The building of training teams or in other words, the building of a network of trainers is very important in a large scale training programme. It is a mechanism to test the efficacy of a new concept in the training field at each of the levels.

At the national level, the CTT, for example, tested the Participatory Rural Appraisal technique and adopted it to be incorporated into the NFLP. The CTT exhaustively discusses and practises micro-teaching techniques on the reading, writing, numerals, development activities and income-generation activities to ensure their applicability in the field before they are incorporated into the teaching programme. In the event of a change in government policy, it is the CTT that appreciates and updates the primers and training contents.

The TOT programme adopted for the NFLP has its advantages. It creates a common identity among trainers drawn from various organizations in the country. It promotes a sense of solidarity among members who develop a code of ethics, values and a common understanding of their responsibilities. The training of trainers programme builds confidence among members and reinforces the belief that they acquire special skills to advance the development of the programme and society at large. More importantly, it is a cost effective way of training large groups of people. Its ripple effects are felt at the grassroots level where large groups of people are educated. It produces and makes available a strategic resource of trainers who can be called upon at any time to share their experiences, update their skills, monitor and support the programme at each level.

We now take a close look at the operations of the NFED in one of the regions of Ghana namely, the Western Region.

The Operations of NFED in the Western Region of Ghana

The Western Region is made up of 11 districts. The regional headquarters is the twin-city of Sekondi/Takoradi. District Offices of NFED are located in all the 11 districts of the region.

Reading Centres

An important feature of the programme in the region is the establishment of reading centres to service the literacy classes. These are centres that are established to assist the new literates in their reading endeavours in order to minimize relapse into illiteracy. However, because they have been established in the communities and are stocked with basic reading materials some school children also benefit from them. They are established in the following districts and communities in the Western Region:

Shama Ahanta East: Shama Community, Beposo Community

Wassa Amenfi: Mumuni Camp, Breman, Samreboi, Surano

Wassa West: Prestea, Nsuaem

Batches 6 and 7 classes

Since the programme effectively took off the ground, seven batches of classes have been successfully organized in the Western Region. Two batches of classes, batches 6 and 7 passed out in 1999. The discussion below is based on batches 6 and 7 classes organized in the region.

Table 6:1

Comparative figures of batches 6 and 7 classes

Batch No.	No. of Supervisors	No. of Classes	Facilitators			Enrolment		
			M	F	T	M	T	T
6	127	724	632	92	724	6358	10915	17273
7	127	802	696	106	802	7266	12255	19521
Total	254	1526	1328	198	1562	13624	23170	36794

Compiled from 2000 NFED Western Region Report, Sekondi

It is gratifying to note from Table 6.1 that the number of female learners in both batches exceeded that of males. Almost two thirds (63.3%) were females while only a third were males in batch 6. The scenario was not very different in batch 7. While the male participation was 37.2 per cent female participation was 62.8 per cent. Women continue to actively take part in the classes.

Participation of many women in the programme is an important breakthrough for the educational system because the traditional beliefs which debar many women from attending school appears to have been demystified to some extent by the programme. The educated women will now have a more meaningful role to play in the economic, social and political lives of the community.

The report pointed out that 1003 people dropped out of the class in batch 6. Although the intake in batch 7 increased, only 157 (0.7 per cent) dropped out in batch 7. People were realizing the importance of the programme and are getting committed to it. Reasons advanced for the drop-out rate were mentioned as tiredness after the normal hard work on the farm, family problems, poverty, migration, and lack of interest because they did not see their way clear in employment. Some of the facilitators and learners, the report noted, migrated to take employment in the mining business which was thriving in the region. (The majority of mining companies operate in the Western Region and have become attractive for the youth in the face of unemployment and economic hardships).

In addition to the rural newspapers published at the NFED national headquarters, each district published its own local news to provide post literacy materials to encourage learners to continue to read and write. The most regular among these publications was the *Western Star* published by the Nzema East District. The 13th Edition of *Western Star* (Sept.1999) discussed in detail the advantages of family life education. Couples were advised to space their children and be responsible citizens and parents. The problems created by religious conflict due to the introduction of Sharia Law in Nigeria were referred to. Learners were advised to avoid any religious conflicts that might bring disaster into the country. The editorial of the edition was on population census. Attention of readers was drawn to the importance of the census which was on-going.

Communities were educating themselves through the publication of their own newspapers. These papers were read in the classes and discussed. Jomoro District extensively and appropriately used cartoons and sketches to attract the attention of learners to serious discussions. Avenues were created for the local people to educate themselves through the print media.

The collaboration of NFED with some organizations in the region has yielded much fruit. For example collaboration with the Ministry of Agriculture projects have drawn the youth into agriculture under the Youth in Agriculture Programme. The Ministry of Agriculture was able to provide training and inputs to learners to help increase food production targets in the region. Some of the agricultural centres established by NFED under the Youth in Agriculture Programme are shown below:

Table 6.2

Youth in Agriculture Programme

District	Name of class	Crop	Acreage
Waasa West	Ningo community	Okro	5
	Wassa Aimpa Apostolic Class	Rice	6
	Fantakrom Literacy Class	Rice	5
	Koranteng Krom Literacy Class	Rice	4
	Tukyinantia Class	Rice	5
	Obengkrom Class	Cowpea	2
Aowin Suaman	Aduyakorm Class	Rice	2
Sefwi-Wiaso	Ntrentreso Class	Garden eggs	2
	Bosomoiso Class	Onion	2
	Boako Literacy Class	Rice	4
Jomoro	Nyame Kwame	Piggery	29 pigs

Complied from 2000 NFED Western Region Report, Sekondi

Table 6.2 shows that a variety of crops and vegetables were cultivated. The report submitted alongside the Table notes that the youth in particular have taken advantage of the training and inputs provided to become farmers. They have been able to produce food crops and animals for sale and for their own consumption. Their lifestyles began to change as they became responsible for themselves and others. Some of them claimed that they married because of income generated from the farming activities. They were more able to look after their wards in schools. An encouraging aspect of the agricultural programme was that the majority of the participants fell within the active productive group. They promised to continue working in the agricultural sector because of the appropriate techniques they acquired during the period. They accepted the challenge to produce not only for their consumption but also for export.

The report explains that a group in the Wassa West district had constructed a cocoa shed and applied to the Ghana Cocoa Board to purchase their cocoa. A purchasing clerk was needed and their facilitator was appointed and trained as one. They were happy because they were not cheated as some other purchasing clerks used to do. They were motivated to produce more cocoa for the world market.

Shama, the facilitator in Nyamekwame, established a piggery and benefited from the Youth in Agriculture loan. Shama won the Best Farmer Award in piggery in the Jomoro District. This boosted the morale of learners to take up piggery in the district. Piggery has become a popular pastime in the district. Pig farmers sold their produce to their neighbours.

A church class in Ningo in the Wassa West District was able to generate funds under the income-generating activity to roof their chapel, purchase a set of musical instruments, some benches, a wall clock and some lanterns for the church. The church now attracts a large congregation who live together in a friendly environment.

It was also noted that NFED in the Western Region entered into a collaboration with SNV (Ghana) a Netherlands-based NGO in 1996 for support of its programmes. The collaboration was in the areas of family life, literacy and education. The SNV provided a public address system which was used in public education programmes in the Mpohor Wassa East District. It provided equipment to the same district to desilt and clean gutters and drains. It also made funds and materials available for the training of Community Based Distributors (CBDs) to educate community members on population and family planning issues. It made condoms and other contraceptives like the pill available to users. The necessary education on AIDS, reproductive health and family planning techniques which are global issues, were adequately given to the people. SNV has also adopted seven all-female literacy classes in the district and provided them with gas lamps.

Consequently, many people have begun to plan their families and cater for their children more adequately. It was reported that patients in the Mpohor Wassa East District have resorted to receiving treatment from the Ahmaddiya Mission Hospital at Daboase instead of consulting witch doctors or attributing the causes of sickness to old ladies and to the vengeance of the gods (Western Region NFED Report 2000).

The SNV supported the programme with resources for the training of 65 facilitators and 12 supervisors who were each provided with a bicycle and a motor bike respectively. Thus, facilitation and supervision of the classes were effective. Radios, lanterns, gas lamps and exercise books were provided by SNV to enhance class progress. Learners listened to news items from the regions, the districts and from the world. They have developed the interest in knowing what happened not only in their communities but also in other societies.

The results of these collaborative programmes are that the environment has been kept clean, people have become more aware of their rights and responsibilities and planned their families. They can also read and write, form productive co-operatives as is noted at Senchem and Nkwaabaa where learners keep records and transact business with the banks.

Other organizations that the functional literacy programme in the Western Region collaborated with include the Community Water and Sanitation Project. This has led to the provision of potable water in many communities. The Population Council, the Commission on Human Rights and Administrative Justice, the Ghana Education Service and other non-governmental organizations have readily worked with organized groups of learners formed by the NFED. The learners discussed issues about safe water, clean environment, world population issues and human rights

It has been reported that many leaders emerged from the classes to organize community development programmes like school building. They also kept their compounds neat. Some learners became very interested in reading the Bible. Both Christians and non-Christians read the Bible because, as they claimed, they appreciated the stories and the morals they provided. The neo-literates in the churches in the Jomoro District have for instance, intensified the reading of the Bible in Nzema. They could also sing from the hymnbooks in the local language. The days of humming hymns, singing only the first stanza which was known by the majority of the congregation, or repeating the choruses were also over. Moreover, the officiating minister did not read aloud the songs while the congregation sangs. Learners could now read as they sang.

They accepted religious responsibilities willingly and contributed positively towards the success of church activities such as harvests, anniversaries and communal work (Western Region Report 2000).

Learners have been encouraged to form co-operatives and undertake income-generating activities. These groups have been granted soft loans to operate their businesses, they have been trained by the NBSSI and appropriate agencies as determined by NFED through collaboration. Table 6.3 below shows some of the income-generation co-operatives which benefited from credit facilities.

Table 6:3 shows that 12 groups undertook income-generation activities to earn income. A more satisfying aspect of their business was the variety of projects they worked on. These included gari processing, fish smoking, soyabean bread making, soap making and wheat bread making. Others were piggery, pottery and palm oil extraction. After the initial training some members established their own small-scale industries to produce for the open market. The focus was on agro-based small-scale industries since agricultural production has great potential for the economic expansion of Ghana. The importance of the loan is that it serves as an incentive which beneficiaries never expected to get in their lives. Now they handle and count more money than ever before. Moreover, it is not just credit but a credit with education. They learn to properly manage their various trades so as to minimize losses and maximize profits. The situation makes a lot of different in their lives and makes them proud.

The loan, one might think, was not enough. But the commitment of the people accounted for the success of the projects. It is explained by the report that many of the groups paid their loans and generated their own capital to expand the project or undertake other activities. It was reported that the Homorkorpe Literacy Group for instance was able to sink a well to the tune of ¢200,000.00 from gari making. They now have regular access to good drinking water. Many of the bakers now bake without external financial assistance. The same applies to the gari producers and oil extractors. They are self-sufficient in the goods they produce and employ others to work with them to produce for the community and their neighbours.

108

Table 6.3

Income-Generation Groups under the Second phase of NFED Credit Scheme
January 1998-December, 1999

No.	Name of Group	District	Project	Loan Given (¢)
1	Aboa Gardens	Ahanta West	Palm Oil Ext.	1,400,000
2.	Homorkope Community	Shama Ahanta East	Gari Making	500,000
3.	Bronikrom Community	Shama Ahanta East	Gari Making	500,000
4.	Surona Saviour Church	Bibiani A Bekwai	Soap making	600,000
5.	Agbesinyale Community	Jomoro	Bakery	1,100,000
6.	Kwaabaa Community	Mpohor Wassa East	Gari making	1,300,000
7.	Apprasuegye Community	Sefwi Wiawso	Piggery	900,000
8.	Bechiwa Mangoase	Sefwi Wiawso	Pottery	600,000
9.	Mumuni Camp Community	Wassa Amenfi	Palm Oil Ext.	1,300,000
10.	Teiku Agave	Wassa Amenfi	Gari making	1,300,000
11.	Epoku Catholic Class	Jomoro	Bakery	1,100,000
12.	Bibiani Christ Revival	Bibiani A Bekwai	Soyabean Bread	1,200,000
Total				¢12,800,00

Compiled from *2000 NFED Western Region Report, Sekondi*

The learning groups, however, experienced some problems. The rural newspapers were irregular in some communities. It was also pointed out that some facilitators were more interested in reading and discussing aspects of the programme in classes than in teaching the people numeracy and writing. This discouraged learners as they became fed up with the same processes at the expense of the other aspects of learning namely, numeracy and writing which they thought would help them calculate and record their business transactions. Some learners also withdrew because they were fed up with reading their local language materials most of the time as materials in English were difficult to get at some centres. On the whole however, there were happy indications that the programme was able to mobilize people to improve upon their living standards. Job opportunities were created for the youth and development of communities has been initiated.

Quite apart from the above-mentioned groups, the Division supported the activities of other groups in the informal sector. Non-formal educational activities were organized for barbers, truck pushers, hairdressers, tailors and seamstresses, carpenters and masons. Other groups supported in the informal industrial sector by the educational programmes were gold-and black-smiths, potters, petty traders and "chop-bar" keepers. The artisans learnt to record particulars of their creditors, manage their businesses, operate accounts with rural banks, form co-operatives and learnt together. Artisans were supported to form co-operatives to promote their own activities and fight for good prices and rights. Indications were that all the groups supported by the programme were performing better than before. They expressed the desire to continue working with the NFED as long as her facilities and services are available.

It is becoming increasingly clear that training has become a necessary condition for economic growth in rural areas. The rural industry is growing fast and has the capacity of absorbing many individuals who may not be able to secure wage-earning jobs in the formal sector. The unemployed and the semi-skilled learn some trade and establish their own small-scale ventures. In the literacy classes, people learn about modern trends in the global economy and discuss at the local level what they can also do to become players at their level.

A welcome result of the programme is the dignity that is given to women in society. The focus of the programme is on the development of women. It is, therefore, not surprising that, women constitute the majority of learners. They actively take part in the income-generation activities and claim to have become better home managers. They are happy to recognize the importance of vegetables and fruits in food preparation and service.

The civic education messages relayed by the public address system and the support given by the National Commission for Civic Education (NCCE) in Mpohor Wassa East created civic awareness in the district. It was noted in the district that, people now willingly took part in communal labour. They were also able to construct school buildings and dig wells. The essence of community ownership and maintenance of these projects was nurtured by the people. They discussed local and international issues confidently. They easily discussed the trend of the global market in relation to the fall in the price of cocoa and the effects of the high cost of oil in recent years. Now, they have begun to understand the importance of the world economy and the roles expected of them to play.

The general comments from learners in the field have shown that the project met with success. Those engaged in the income-generation activities especially in gari making at Teiku Agave and Mpohor Wassa East claimed that now that they could read figures on tickets they were no longer cheated by tax collectors. They were happy that they were linked to banking institutions like Women's World Banking and to organizations like Technoserve, NBSSI, Ghana National Poverty Reduction Programme and Empretec. At their own level, they wrote proposals to these organizations for support. They were exposed to modern patterns of business transactions and the competition in the open market with others. They could produce enough for the family and market their surplus produce.

Communities in Shama Ahanta East, especially, were happy that they had become more aware of personal and environmental issues. They learnt to wash their hands with soap before eating, learnt to cover their food and wash utensils immediately after meals. They kept their surroundings neat and managed their household waste better. They learnt to plant trees and harvest the grown ones more judiciously. Indiscriminate bush burning was minimized. They also learnt about the need to join the rest of the world to fight against degradation and pollution. They showed commitment in the implementation of the programme. A sense of ownership of projects was nurtured and the groups took communal responsibility of these projects. They were thus able to sustain them.

Another prominent outcome of the programmes was that the majority of learners began to use wristwatches. The youth among them especially appreciated the ownership of watches and admitted that they had become time-conscious as they started using watches. Some explained that their status had been enhanced in their communities because they could write and read their own letters. The curiosity to read other materials was created. They brought pressure to bear on organizations like the District Assemblies and government institutions such as the Ministries of Agriculture and Health to satisfy some pressing demands, an action they could not have taken before the NFED programme started.

The programme also empowered the people to participate in the political issues of the community. Indeed, people have begun to reject politicians who have not lived up to expectation. The Member of Parliament for the Sekondi Constituency in the Western Region who won the parliamentary seat in 1992 at the beginning of the literacy programme, and was a Deputy Minister for Interior lost his seat in 1996. This was when the literacy programme was in full gear. The electorate asserted that they were empowered by the programme to critically assess issues and the performance of those in power. They explained that now that they are empowered by the NFED, they would vote wisely in the 2004 elections. The results would reflect how literacy has empowered them politically.

One commendable achievement of the programme is the graduation of some participants from the literacy classes to the formal school system. A few examples from the Northern Region of Ghana are provided in Table 6:4 below

Table 6.4

Graduation from Literacy Class to the Formal School System

NO.	District	Basic Education	SecondCycle	Tertiary
1	Tamale	48	8	2
2	Tolon/Kumbungu	24	0	0
3	Bole	15	10	0
4	Saboba/Chereponi	14	0	2
5	Zabzugu/Tatale	13	1	0
6	Yendi	7	3	1
7	East Mamprusi	5	17	1
8	Gushegu/Karaga	5	5	0
9	Savelugu/Nanton	3	4	0
	Total	134	46	6

Compiled from Northern Region NFED 2001 Report, Tamale

Table 6.4 reveals some promising results of the literacy classes in terms of graduation to the formal system of education from nine districts in the Northern Region. One hundred and eighty-six graduated from literacy classes to advance to various levels in the formal school system. Out of this number 134 were in various primary schools in the region. Forty-six of them were attending second cycle institutions while six entered tertiary institutions to pursue a variety of courses. It is worthwhile mentioning the names and particulars of the six in tertiary institutions. Suleman Abukari from the Sanga Literacy class in the Tamale Municipality was pursuing a course in Tamale Polytechnic. From the same literacy class Pastor Stephen was attending Sanga Bible School. Adam Issahaku has also graduated from the Gbintin Literacy class in the East Mamprusi District and entered Tamale Polytechnic. John Nteche of the Saboba literacy class was pursuing a Bible Study programme in Kumasi. It is gratifying and inspiring to note the academic ambition of Munkaila Adams. With his background studies at Bang Berisung literacy class in the Yendi District he was then an undergraduate student of the University for Development Studies, Tamale.

Since it is a common knowledge that education is the bedrock of development, it is hoped that the educated who graduate from the non-formal education to the formal system at al levels will use their expertise to promote rural development.

Acquisition and Use of Numeracy Skills

In this global environment of rapid change, numeracy becomes an essential feature in non-formal education's drive to strengthen the potentials of adults. Numeracy is important because it forms part of the daily transactions of the adult. Much emphasis is, therefore, placed on the teaching of numeracy skills in Ghana's literacy programme. The results of teaching literacy in the classes are rewarding.

In the social setting, the beneficiary of non-formal education programme uses numeracy in searching for radio and television stations and in dialing telephone numbers on both mobile and fixed phones. Literacy helps him to read dates, calendars and prescriptions on drugs.

In the economic sphere, the adult uses numeracy in the market and other economic and occupational transactions. He is no longer engaged in the barter system of trade, nor does he depend on others to check his money for him. Numeracy enhances his budgeting, calculation of profit and loss margins and recording his debtors and creditors. More importantly, he has access to credit facilities which he can sign for. He deals with his bankers directly without the resort to others in filling forms or signing his bank documents. He learns to count the number of items sold or quantity of crops planted or harvested. He learns about weighing his crops and foodstuffs such as cocoa, gari and sheanuts in kilograms. He also learns to measure his crops and farmlands and take the length and height in metres as appropriate. Extension officers, middlemen and women, labourers and buying clerks, no longer easily cheat him. The adult woman can now read the weight of her children at the weighing centres.

As far as money transactions are concerned, the adult worker is able to calculate and record huge sums of money accurately. He also learns to handle currencies carefully and more frequently, saves in the banks.

On the whole, the neo-literate could read, write and calculate figures related to his life and work. He could work with mathematical operational signs (addition (+), subtraction (–), division (÷), multiplication (x) and equal to (=). He was able to work with relatively high numbers in his transactions.

Generally speaking, many parents who benefited from the programme realized the importance of education. They, therefore, sent their children to school. Many participants formed co-operatives and undertook income-generating activities. Community and environmental improvement activities like the construction of market sheds, schools, street drains, forestation and wells have been undertaken. People were committed to do things in new ways. They began to face the challenges of the fast changing world (NFED 1999b).

The work of Ghana's Non-formal Education Division has shown how a well executed national adult education programme can draw people's attention to national and international issues so that they can meaningfully participate in the new development process. It has led to the integration of rural people into the main stream of social and economic lives of their communities. It has contributed to realization of the vision of poverty reduction, employment creation and improvement in rural incomes.

Chapter 7

SOME BARRIERS TO NON-FORMAL EDUCATION

The author does not pretend that non-formal education (NFE) is a miraculous panacea which has no barriers and inherent weaknesses and can readily solve all development problems. If it were so, many poor and struggling countries would have developed at an unprecedented rate by making use of non-formal education. There are various factors which impede the progress of NFE. Some of these barriers are discussed below.

The Government Will

The crucial factor limiting the progress of non-formal education in many countries is the national "muscle". Where there is the national political will, non-formal education programmes are likely to succeed. The political will can not function in isolation. It needs to have:

1) support of the civil service (implementers), else the political statements become just rhetoric and nothing is implemented;

2) an administrative system to translate the political statement into tangible programmes e.g. A Department of NFE with adequately qualified staff to arrange programmes (training, monitoring and evaluation);

3) strong political vision and direction; In this case, non-formal education must be defined in terms of national goals and given official, moral, financial and technical support. This has been the case in Tanzania when the government of Julius Nyerere pooled all human and material resources together to support non-formal education. All means of communication were harnessed to whip

up enthusiasm among those who had weak educational motivation. The government planned NFE properly and it succeeded. The example is just one of the few exceptions. The current NFE programme in Ghana also has strong political vision and direction.

As Paulo Freire and Julius Nyerere pointed out, non-formal education is the transfer of power to the majority of people. It thus has the power to liberate. Though non-formal education may have the capacity to liberate, it invariably takes place within an ideological frame-work. Like all forms of education, it is not value-free. Education is a social as well as a political institution. Leaders are often scared and protest, in one form or the other, against programmes dealing with power distribution when they pose a threat to the *status quo*. As a result, those in authority watch the activities of non-formal educators with eagle eyes with a view to putting them under lock and key should the educators shake the political barometer. Paulo Freire was stripped of his Brazilian citizenship because he was giving too much power to the people. When the New Patriotic Party government of John Agyekum Kufour took over the reins of government from the National Democratic Congress of John Jerry Rawlings in 2001, the activities of NFED were temporarily put on hold in the name of a restructuring exercise. However, NFE which is established just to carry out government policies without taking the local people into partnership is lame. The liberation of people to participate in personal and community development is the educators' mission. Educators must, therefore, not lose sight of their mission and sing politicians' tune.

Liberators can only use the non-formal education process in two ways to achieve their objectives:

1. by operating cleverly but openly within the margins allowed by the authorities who have power. In the developed countries like Britain, those margins are very wide because the value system is fairly open and pluralistic. In the developing countries, the margins are usually narrow as they were in Brazil.

117

2. by going under-ground and concentrating on working gradually from within. In sum, all the best teachers actually do both in all countries to liberate people.

Change of Government

The frequent coups d'etat and instability in the developing world retard the progress of NFE programmes. Some politicians openly argue that one does not complete another's building. They have to model the educational system to suit their political ends. This accounts for the frequent establishment of education committees all over the continent. Committee members invite a small number of people to a series of seminars, pushing their ideology through to plan for non-formal education. They usually come up with a document on non-formal education on the advice of foreign consultants who may not be well abreast with local conditions. There will be no commitment from the beneficiaries of this programme especially when non-formal education administration is centralized at national head office and very distant from the people. Unfortunately, this is usually the case.

Individual and Group Attitude

Some individuals and groups have their own tastes, identification and values. They tend to have different views about NFE. There is a wide range of interest in choice and rejection of non-formal education programmes and organizations. This is compounded by the fact that the individual developing countries have not as yet developed any national character. People referred to as conservatives and who call themselves "old guards" in Ghana for instance, do not want to learn anything new or welcome any change. Among them are some politicians and traditional rulers. Their argument is that an old dog cannot learn new tricks. The influence wielded by these groups of people is strong and can be a great source of embarrassment to the educator. They may, therefore, not accept NFE programmes which bring change.

There are also the complacent including some traders, traditional-ists, farmers and the old generation of teachers who are content with the old methods they have been using over the years. They believe that since those methods have sustained them, they are the best and must be maintained. They have, therefore, not much to do with non-formal education which they perceive will make their job more difficult should they learn new issues.

The cynics are also suspicious of anything that will bring change and they will not support non-formal education programmes. These are the businessmen, the technicians and craftsmen of all categories (tailors, carpenters, woodworkers, craftsmen, blacksmith) who will not appreciate it if many products of non-formal education infiltrate into their occupational ranks. They see non-formal education as a threat to their livelihood. Their attitude, therefore, scares off the youth from join-ing their ranks.

Behaviour of Non-Formal Educators

The behaviour of some non-formal educators also leaves much to be desired. Some do not have a sense of commitment required for the type of work they are expected to do. They value their position as a mark of class distinction separating the holder like a gold medal, from those who have not got it. They lord it over learners, undermine their intelligence, drive in posh cars or ride on motor-bikes with disregard for learners. They lead ostentatious lives at times, while advising par-ticipants to go back to the land, work in cottage and rural industries or to remain in the rural area which lacks many social amenities. Often the clientele suspect the motives of these educators. Too much suspicion leads to loss of confidence in the educators. Although learners are aware that most of the educators are not interested in them but in their own welfare, they have no choice but to look for direction from their "masters". This may not be their stand in all cases. At times, they advise themselves on the steps to take.

119

Problems of Adults

Adult participants have many problems which prevent them from regular participation in programmes even if they are interested in them. They may be parents, church elders, office holders in many social, economic or political associations. They may be husbands or wives with families and may be experiencing some of the problems associated with aging such as general physical weakness, poor eyesight and defective hearing. They may have the burning desire to participate fully in the programmes, but may be handicapped by these problems.

The Extended Family Network

In traditional African society, people's survival depends on the solidarity of the extended family. The lineage shares a common cooking pot (meals), a common farm, craft and trade (budget) and a common house (residence). The extended family has undergone tremendous changes since colonialism. In most African countries, the nuclear family has become the production and consumption unit though the regime of social solidarities within the extended family has not fully disappeared. The problem of one member is thus the problem of the whole lineage. Relatives must participate in funerals, festivals, marriages, court proceedings, customary rites and social functions of the lineage and its members. They must take part in games, cultural entertainment, and leisure activities such as hunting, honey-collection, brewing of local drinks or tapping of palm wine. These have been designed to ensure the stability of society and cohesion of the extended family system.

In rural Ghana, the status of a person in the lineage and the community is determined by his social role and participation in these activities. Adults do not then have time to themselves, as children do in the formal school system, to participate in non-formal education programmes. This is a serious setback to non-formal education. Participants are not readily available for the programmes at all times. At best, they arrive late or break and miss the trend of lessons. Non-formal education programmes can not have the impact that they are designed for under these circumstances.

Problems of Acquisition and Utilization of Skills and Knowledge

Though non-formal education has the capacity to help solve develop-ment problems, the process of acquiring skills is in itself not all that simple as one may wish to believe. The educational programme may be drawn with the best of intentions, yet participants may not fully accept or implement what is conveyed to them. This may be due to several reasons. One of the reasons is that some people are afraid of freedom and responsibility and may not like to fight for and accept their rights though NFE could be used to persuade them to do so.

Dewey (1916) also points out that the success of the education process is largely determined by inborn qualities or the organs of students. These organs, he explains, are conditioned to operate in different ways such that, though they may be changed by education, "the notion of a spontaneous normal development of these activities (organs) is pure mythology" (*Ibid* 133). Individuals have their distinctive temperaments which cannot easily be changed in the way expected by the educator. Change in the individual may also be at different stages. In view of the above, Dewey states that "the strong biased human organ becomes "limiting factors in all education; they do not furnish its ends or aims" (*Ibid*.: 133). The objectives of the education process are rarely realized among adult learners, especially where the literacy level is low.

All education like non-formal education is to bring change in the beliefs, behaviour, knowledge and skills in people for self-sufficiency and community improvement. But change can be very painful when one has to substitute, or abandon his developed set of values and skills. The pain of going through change differs from person to person. Change can be as painful as child birth. Many people may not like to experi-ence this pain for long.

Levels of Adoption of Change

An old Euro-American research which has some relevance for us, has shown how ideas are transferred and adopted with some pain in the community. This research reveals that it takes 15 years for an innovative idea to be fully accepted by almost all the people. This research finding comes up with a model of a process of adoption of ideas known as the "Adaptation-Adoption Process". This model has categorized six types of adopters. These are:

1. Five per cent (5%) Innovators: Only 5 per cent of people readily accept and try new ideas for themselves and are high risk takers.

2. Fifteen percent (15%) Adapters: They are the people who see the potential benefits of the innovation and want it introduced and see it work. They are also high risk takers.

3. Thirty per cent (30%) Early Adopters: They realize the need for change after listening and observing the Adapters for some time. They see and want benefits of change and are medium risk takers.

4. Thirty per cent (30%) Adopters: They hear about the benefits of the innovation and want to enjoy the benefits but at the same time, they adhere to folklore and are low risk takers.

5. Fifteen (15%) Slow Adopters: They adhere more strongly to local norms. They accept the innovation because it is widely spread and accepted. They take no risks at all in accepting the innovation.

6. Five per cent (5%) Laggards: They strongly believe that the best way to do things is the old way. They may not accept the change at all.

This model shows that it is difficult for many people to accept change immediately. With a diversity of techniques and with the support of the media (as discussed earlier) a well planned and relevant non-formal education programme will reduce the time frame to one year or little more, for the majority of people to adopt to change. One must not lose sight of the good incentives and rewards attached to the programme.

Reward System

Rewards and prestige attached to the work of graduates of the non-formal education system are not attractive enough. The products of the formal system are engaged in white-collar jobs with higher salaries in the urban centres while graduates of the non-formal system are employed on blue-collar or typical traditional jobs with lower incentives in the rural setting.

Thus, people are suspicious of the non-formal education idea. They conclude that it is one of those tricks of beneficiaries of "the White man's education" to condemn the rural folk to inferior jobs in the rural area. They prefer to learn English which they believe is the language of the modern scholar. Many, therefore, prefer to acquire the same "first class" education for themselves and their children. There is, therefore, pressure from society for the integration of the two systems (formal and non-formal education) so that participants can transfer from one to the other or that similar programmes can be mounted in both institutions. This has been the case in Ghana when many liberal education centres of the Institute of Adult Education were turned into GCE course centres in 1962. This was the origin of the Workers' Colleges of the Institute of Adult Education of the University of Ghana.

There is also the pressure from people and tendency by authorities to formalize non-formal education programmes. The Village Polytechnics of Kenya and the Folk Development Colleges in Tanzania stand this danger. Their products even use their qualification to look for employment in the urban area instead of "going private". The pressure for integration and formalization, therefore, has serious implications for the progress of non-formal education which has specific goals, structure, course content, target groups and educators with their identity and skills. Julius Nyerere tried to give support to non-formal education by bridging the remuneration gaps between all categories of workers. Importance is attached to whatever responsible work the citizens were engaged in and links were established between both formal and non-formal education institutions. The classrooms, the same teachers and at times, the same textbooks of the school system were used for non-formal education programmes.

Resource Materials

A crucial dilemma facing non-formal education programme is the production of resource materials. Some have been written at the national level by educational planners and experts. The baseline studies for the preparation of primers and charts are limited in the sense that their collection is influenced by "experts". Many of the interpretations are projections of the experts on what ought to be. The only part the local people play is to provide baseline information which might not even be accurately recorded or analyzed. The materials may be cleverly manipulated to provide correct answers to questions the planners have. Attention may be diverted from social, economic and political structures which suppress people and place them in the culture of silence and suffering. Poor salaries, bad roads, high cost of living and unjust social and political institutions are not treated. But these are issues NFE must address. Materials consist of what the government wants learners to read. They read about advantages derived from the use of fertilizer, modern methods of farming, payment of taxes, family planning, respect for authority and balanced diet. The educator uses these existing materials to perpetuate the culture of silence. They teach learners that they are poor because they are illiterate forgetting that poverty, lack of educational opportunities and suppression have made them illiterate.

The use of these resource materials means compromising with some of the basic principles of the non-formal system. Participants become passive consumers of materials which may not be appropriate for them but satisfy the aspirations of the ruling class. The local people can be given the necessary training to collect and collate their resource materials. In so doing, they actively engage in thinking, planning, reflecting and acting. These are techniques which are essential features of the non-formal education process.

Non-Formal Education Institutions

Many developing countries have embarked upon non-formal education programmes. Yet, they lack institutions which are committed to the training of non-formal educators and beneficiaries who will be proud to associate themselves with NFE professionals. These institutions must be reorganized and recognized as the central point of community and national development. Non-formal education institutions like the Folk Development Colleges in Tanzania, Village Polytechnics in Kenya, Folk High Schools in the Scandinavian countries and the Land Grant Universities in the U.S.A. which periodically bring non-formal educators together are lacking in most countries which claim to be using non-formal education for development. In some cases, non-formal education administrators are selected from the ranks of politicians and teachers loyal to the ruling party. Facilitators, supervisors and evaluators are party functionaries.

What they succeed in doing is to promote the teaching of the ideas of the ruling government so that they can maintain their positions. Non-formal education is not treated fairly.

Knowledge Base of Non-Formal Education

The other problem is that, at present, the knowledge-base of non-formal education is very weak. Qualified extension officers in the field who practise non-formal education are few. Many others including those who are naturally gifted in their vocations especially in the crafts have low academic standards and low technical know-how in facilitating or implementing non-formal education programmes. Those who pass through the formal system have been given inadequate training for a short period of time to prepare them to work with the marginalized. Their knowledge is, therefore, insufficient to effectively work with their clientele. More so, they lack the adult education skills to impart their knowledge to people who are many and isolated in the rural areas.

At this juncture, it has to be emphasized that the participation of universities and especially, university-based adult education institutions in non-formal education is very important. Universities are concerned with teaching, research and service to the community. University-based adult education institutions with their expertise must, therefore, be involved in non-formal education activities to strengthen the knowledge base of NFE programmes. University departments can open training programmes for extension officers of all categories. Non-formal education should not be left in the hands of officials of extension departments of Ministries, party functionaries, revolutionary organs, national service personnel or voluntary associations. They cannot effectively handle non-formal programmes. Universities must adopt participatory research and evaluation approaches to non-formal education programmes and make research reports available and meaningful to people. Non-formal education is a profession which must be handled by adult education professionals.

In summary, it could be said that some of the problems which retard the progress of non-formal education are the national muscle, the family and aging problems of prospective participants, individual and group values, and the complexities surrounding the concept. Despite these barriers the non-formal educator should not resign himself to a state of despondency. He needs to commit himself to work tactfully within the margins that he has at his disposal and make the best out of the situation.

Chapter 8

SUMMARY AND CONCLUSIONS

SUMMARY

The foregoing chapters point out some of the problems of development that have been plaguing many countries. After independence, there developed a decreased certainty of employment and popular participation in community and national development. Political instability and economic structural weaknesses are also identified as serious problems which retard the progress of development in the developing economies.

With time, however, governments attempted to tackle these problems. The top-down model of development with its deficiencies has been abandoned. The bottom-up strategy is adopted with emphasis on catering for the rural poor who have been marginalized as far as the main trend of development is concerned.

It is good to know that change is inevitable. Modern society has become very complex, dynamic and interdependent because of technological innovations. The world has become a global village and all countries are to play their part to make the global process a reality. Globalization demands of all categories of people and nations no matter where they are, to develop skills and knowledge to contribute to the phenomenal change. Globalization also embraces economic development whereby traditional techniques in production are improved to exploit scientific knowledge which, in turn, promotes non-traditional exports. Developing countries need to organize themselves through education to strengthen their participation in the process. They should not stand isolated or as islands outside the global village. Non–formal education is, therefore, a necessity to prepare people and especially the rural people for the process. It is against this background that countries like Brazil, Tanzania and Ghana have embarked upon non-formal education programmes.

CONCLUSION

The Government

The biggest development institution in any country is the government. Where there is the national political will, non-formal education programmes may succeed. It is, therefore, very necessary that the government, its departments and other institutions must be the pivot for development. They must identify the real problem of development, have a clear vision and direction and find appropriate solutions to these problems through non-formal education programmes.

Beneficiaries

If development in the developing world is to progress, it must start from the rural areas where the majority of people live and from where natural resources are tapped. Popular participation in the three stages of non-formal education namely planning, implementation and evaluation must be encouraged. Token forms of participation whereby the minority, especially top civil servants are consulted and decisions taken for the majority must be abandoned. Popular participation changes the structures which impede progress.

The Facilitator and the Administrator

The central figure in the non-formal education programme is the facilitator. The facilitator should not adopt the attitude of paternalism or charisma per se, and believe that he has the preserve of knowledge. In this sense, therefore, the facilitator and the administrator should not impose a package of knowledge or materials on the people.

128

The democratic philosophy of non-formal education, where learners are involved in all stages of the learning process, is implemented. The needs and concerns of learners are considered in the process. Learners are made aware of their inadequacies and what to gain from the educational programme. The facilitator must give learners the opportunity to experiment and practise the new knowledge acquired. Learners must be given the necessary motivation to learn, develop the spirit of mutual trust and the willingness to accept responsibility. The facilitator needs to put in place two favourable conditions to achieve his objectives. Firstly, he must ensure that the physical facilities at the learning centre are conducive for adult learners. There must be appropriate seats for adult use and the room well ventilated with adequate lighting system. Secondly, the facilitator should promote social relationships between himself and learners, and among learners. He must exhibit qualities to enable every learner feel at home to learn.

Elements of teamwork must run through the facilitator's programmes. It is then that resources, skills and experiences of various institutions and persons can be pooled together to solve development problems. Such co-operation and collaboration will bring the media to support NFE programmes.

For NFE programmes to succeed in solving development problems, the facilitator needs the dedication, zeal and commitment of a missionary. In the face of mounting difficulties confronting NFE, the facilitator and the administrator must nurture a sustained hard-working spirit. He must be fair but firm, tolerant of all shades of opinion, punctual and regular at class. He must be honest and trust-worthy and generally a model to inspire all to achieve the best in life.

Small Scale Enterprises

Small scale enterprise promotion, a component of non-formal education, is very important in the rural development process. As such, there is the need for the reorganization of traditional micro-enterprises such as sheabutter extraction, tailoring, shoe mending, blacksmithing and gari processing. Others include carpentry, masonry, pottery, weaving, soap-making, pito-brewing, palm-wine tapping and farming.

Another important local industry which needs reorganization and modernization is the wood and forestry products processing. This industry includes furniture making, carving, herbal medicine preparation, bamboo processing, basket weaving, charcoal making and sawdust processing. Herbal medicine production centers can be established in collaboration with orthodox medical specialists. The industry has the potential of providing employment opportunities for the youth since Africa still has a stock of a variety of species of trees. The plantation of medicinal plants can also be encouraged.

A very good example of a successful wood processing industry is Kpogas Furniture Works. It started as a small carpentry workshop at Abossey Okai, Accra in 1987. It has since 1995 become a limited liability company located along the Odorkor-Kaneshie highway is well organized into four main departments – Administration, Production, Marketing and Accounts. Its workforce strength consists of 104 apprentices, 63 permanent workers, 25 temporary workers and 15 casual workers. Mr Worlanyo Agbo alias Kpogas, the Managing Director of the industry, has estimated that during their peak period when large orders are received for furniture production, the workforce triples. He claims that because of the great demand for furniture of all types, workers are always busy and are well motivated in kind and in cash.

The industry has specialized in the production of all types of furniture including office, bedroom, living room and garden furniture of various designs and standards. It also produces kitchen cabinet. In recent years, it has provided office furniture to establishments such as Ghana Telecom, Barclays Bank, the Department of Urban Roads and the Ghana Shippers' Council. It has manufactured large quantities of classroom furniture to all Polytechniques in Ghana and large stocks of collapsible examination tables/chairs for the West African Examination Council. According to Kpogas, 136 apprentices have so far graduated as carpenters from his industry. Many of them are well-established successful carpenters with many apprentices working under them. One of these graduates is Mr. Stephen Mensah Agbo of Stepman Furniture fame in the Kwasiman-

Odorkor traffic light neighborhood. Carpentry workshops of some of the graduates of Kpogas are established in suburbs of Accra such as Adenta, Madina and Batsona and in some other regions of Ghana. The wood industry has to be promoted.

Organized female participation in the traditional crafts and micro-enterprises is also very important in the rural industrialization process. Many women are already engaged in these enterprises either as their main or secondary occupation. Some engage in them as their hobby or support relatives at leisure. Yet, they cannot derive the maximum benefit from their labour. Their plight is compounded by the fact that they have responsibilities towards family maintenance in view of the disintegration of the extended family system, increased rate of single parenthood, widowhood, teenage motherhood and migration of men to urban areas in search of jobs.

The global economy is monetized and rural people need access to stable income for sustenance. Yet, local entrepreneurs lack start-up capital, reliable sources of raw materials, appropriate intermediate technology, administrative and organizational abilities and ready markets. It is in view of the above that a vigorous training in non-formal education programmes must be organized for rural entrepreneurs to support local communities to initiate, own and manage industries to create wealth for themselves. Training in micro-enterprise should be well planned and executed so that local entrepreneurs would be enabled to transform their job into a career. In an attempt to provide training opportunities to rural entrepreneurs however, an appropriate training needs assessment must be carried out. The process will enhance the understanding of their work, their environment and market forces. The assessment will serve not only as an input for participatory planning but also as a benchmark for monitoring and a baseline for evaluation.

Micro-Enterprise Training Centres

With the establishment of viable micro-enterprise training centres, it is hoped that the rural development process will positively influence all aspects of rural life. Socially, the rural people will be able to enjoy social mobility, health care facilities and recreational and educational opportunities. Economically, they will earn income to improve upon their lifestyles. Culturally, the new system will bring enlightenment and liberate people from undue reliance on traditional beliefs and superstition. They will become more critical and objective in their thinking and action. They will no longer be shadows of others but managers of their own affairs. The more they are educated, the more likely they will actively take part in the development process.

The Apprenticeship System

Apprenticeship like training is an institution, which must be better organized to accelerate the socio-economic development of the rural areas. This is important because it promotes the development of the potentials and creativity of the youth. It also creates avenues for self-help employment and leads to the improvement of the lifestyles of beneficiaries. It must be developed, maintained and supported by both NGOs and GOs as a necessary social-economic system to interact successfully with the global environment.

For many people in developing countries, the hope for participation in the global process is through non-formal education. Non-formal education becomes a consolation for those who missed the formal education opportunities. It opens avenues for those who dropped out of the school system. It equips participants with working skills, develops their imagination and creativity and updates the skills and knowledge of workers in all fields of human endeavour. It provides a happy moment for those who found the school system an unhappy experience to realize the importance of the education process and build self-esteem. It equips individuals with the powers of independence of thought and perception of values.

Non-formal education is important for the development of rural communities because of the demands of globalization. It provides learning opportunities for them in friendly and familiar environments. This arrangement arouses their interest in learning and builds their confidence in participation. As a result, they make conscious efforts to acquire some skills and knowledge to lead sustainable livelihoods. They are thus able to live in harmony with the environment, engage in viable economic activity, get enough food and function effectively as responsible citizens.

Briefly put, the non-formal education programme provides a leverage to motivate learners in the management of development activities. Many learners have discovered their potentials from their learning experiences and the application of the learning concepts to their lives and working environment. Learners graduate from the state of passivity to that of activity, from ignorance to enlightenment and from narrow interests to broad interests.

Non-formal education, a package of political, social and economic development programme, has the potential to respond to the needs of the changing world. It is generally, perceived as a key in the human and rural development process. The popular notion is that once a person acquires the appropriate functional literacy, the quality of his life is positively influenced. He is empowered to participate in the affairs not only of his immediate environs but also of those of the larger society. It is a necessary catalyst in the development process and should be expanded to cover all areas of human development.

Non-formal education deserves to be given the appropriate attention, planned well and integrated fully into the national education system. It needs to be adequately resourced to support the drive towards the eradication of illiteracy, a major obstacle to rural development. The success of non-formal education will support the rural people to participate in the global development process. At the end of the day, therefore, it is hoped that with appropriate planning and implementation of non-formal education programmes, there will be a ray of hope at the end of the development tunnel. Community members will be provided with skills to participate in the rural, national and global process.

BIBLIOGRAPHY

Asamoa, A.K (2001), *On Social Change in Sub-Saharan Africa: A Guide to the Study of the Process of Social Transformation*, Woeli Publishing Services, Accra.

Bank of Ghana (1999), *Annual Report*, Government of Ghana, Accra

Batten, R.T., (1962), *Training for Community Development: A Critical Study of Method*, Oxford University Press, London.

Blaug, M. (1973), *Education and Employment Problem in Developing Countries*. ILO Office, Geneva .

Boadu-Ayeboafoh, Yaw, (ed, 2002), Daily *Graphic* No. 14798 August 2002, Graphic Communication Group, Accra.

Bown, L and Tomori, S., (1979), *A Handbook of Adult Education for West Africa*, Hutchinson & Company, London.

Briggs, Asa, (1999), *Technology and the Media*, Microsoft Corporation, USA.

Coombs, P., (1968), *The World Education Crisis: A System's Analysis*, OUP, London.

Coombs, P. and M. Ahmed. (1974) *Attacking Rural Poverty: How Non-formal Education Can Help*, Baltimore, Johns Hopkins University Press.

Dewey J., (1916), *Democracy and Education: An Introduction to Philosophy of Education*, Macmillan, New York.

Dore, R., (1976), *The Diploma Disease: Education, Qualification and Development*, Allen and Unwin, London.

135

Dodds T., (1972), *Multi-Media Approaches to Rural Education,* International Extension College, Cambridge.

Dorvlo L.K.T., (1980), *Integrated Approach to Rural Development: A Critical Examination of some Policy Issues Arising from Ghana's Youth and Development Programme,* E.P. Church, Ho.

Fordham P., (1980), (Ed), *Participation. Learning and Change,* Commonwealth Secretariat, London.

Fordham P., (1965), *The Role of Universities in Non-formal Education.* Michigan State University, East Lansing.

Foster, Philip (1965), *Education and Social Change in Ghana,* Routledge and Kegan Paul, London.

Freire, Paulo, (1972), *Pedagogy of the Oppressed,* Pengiun Books Ltd., Harmonsworth.

Freire, Paulo, (1973), *Education the Practice of Freedom*, Writers and Readers Publishing Co-operatives.

Freir, Paulo, (1985), *Education for Critical Consciousness,* Sheed and Ward, London.

Ghana Education Service (1999), *National Education Forum Report,* Accra.

Ghana statistical Service, (2002) *2000 Population and Housing Census,* Ghana Publishing Corporation, Accra.

Harbison, F. H., (1968), The Generation of Employment in Newly Developing Countries, in J.K. Sheffield (ed.) *Education, Employment and Rural Development,* University College, Nairobi.

136

Hinzen, H and Hundsdorfer V. H., (1979), *Education for Liberation and Development*. The Tanzanian Experience, Evans Brothers Ltd., London.

Hope, Anne and Timmel, Sally, (1984), *Training for Transformation: A Handbook for Community Workers,* Mambo Press, Zimbabwe

Illich, Ivan, (1972), *Deschooling Society,* Penguin Book, Hamonsworth.

ISSER, (2000). *The State of the Ghanaian Economy in 1999,* Wilco Publicity Services Limited, Accra.

Kingsey, D.C. and Bing, I.W. (1978), *Non-Formal Education in Ghana.* Centre for International Education (UMASSO), Amherst

Lockard, C. A. (1999), *Seeds of Globalization,* Microsoft Corporation USA.

Longworth, R. (1999), *The New Global Economic Order*, Microsoft Corporation, USA.

Mbiti, J.S, (1977), *African Religions and Philosophy*, Morrison and Gibbs, London.

NCCE, (1999), *Unit Committees,* Leutram Ltd., Accra.

Non-Formal Education Division (1999a), *Literacy Empowerment Through Community Ownership for Sustainability into the Next Millennium,* NFED, Accra.

Non-Formal Education Division (1999b), *NFED at A Glance*, Accra.

Non-Formal Education Division (1999), *NFED Western Regional Report,* Sekondi.

NFED (2001), *NFED Northern Regional Report,* Tamale.

NBSSI, *NBSSI News* Vol. No. 5 (1999), Best Time Press, Accra

Nyerere, J.K., (1976), *Nyerere on Education and Society,* Open University.

Population Reference Bureau, (1995), *World Population Data Sheet,* Washington

Population Reference Bureau, (1999), *World Population Data Sheet,* Washington

Reimer, Everett, (1972), *School is Dead: An Essay on Alternatives in Education,* Penguin Book Ltd., Hardmonsworth.

Republic of Ghana (1992), *The 1992 Republican Constitution,* Assembly Press, Accra.

Sautoy du P, (1960) *Adult Literacy Teaching in Ghana,* Oxford University Press, London.

Sarpong, Peter (1986), *Ghana in Retrospect: Some Aspects of Ghanaian Culture,* Ghana Publishing Corporation, Accra.

Schumacher, E.F (1973), *Small Is Beautiful: A Study of Economics as if People Mattered.* ABACUS, London.

Simkins, T., (1977), *Non-Formal Education for Development,* University of Manchester, Manchester.

Smutylo, J.S (1973), *Apprenticeship in the Wayside of an Accra Neighbourhood.* Unpublished MA Dissertation, Legon.

United Nations Organization (1971), *What It Is, What It Does;* UNO, New York.

World Bank (2202), *Ghana and World Bank: A Partnership for Progress,* World Bank Office, Accra

World Development Report (1999), *1998/1999 Annual Report,* Spur, Washington

INDEX

www.ingramcontent.com/pod-product-compliance
Lightning Source LLC
Chambersburg PA
CBHW021830020426
42334CB00014B/563

9 7 8 9 9 9 6 4 3 0 3 4 2 6